From
Thurmond
to
Wallace

Numan V. Bartley

From
Thurmond
to
Wallace

Political Tendencies in Georgia
1948-1968

The Johns Hopkins University Press
Baltimore and London

The Johns Hopkins University Press, Baltimore, Maryland 21218
The Johns Hopkins University Press Ltd., London

ISBN 0-8018-1170-8 (clothbound edition)
ISBN 0-8018-1555-X (paperbound edition)

Originally published, 1970
Johns Hopkins Paperbacks edition, 1973

Contents

Preface

Southern politics is passing through a period of profound transformation. The emergence of a two-party system, the re-entry of Negroes into the political process, growing voter participation on the part of both white and black citizens, equitable urban-suburban representation in state legislatures—these and other developments offer unmistakable evidence of political change. This work is an attempt to determine how these changes have been integrated into the politics of the state of Georgia. It is intended simply as a monograph on voting tendencies. As such, the main patterns of voter response to the candidates and issues that have confronted Georgia voters in recent years are its central concern, and the narrative has been confined to those matters that seemed necessary to explain voter reaction. The conclusions are not particularly heartening.

The preparation of this study has left me indebted to a number of individuals and institutions. A research fellowship from the Institute of Southern History at The Johns Hopkins University and a grant from the Georgia Tech Foundation made it possible for me to devote uninterrupted attention to this project, and I am grateful.

Among the individuals who have given me much needed assistance, I am most indebted to my wife, Morraine. It would have been more appropriate to list her as co-author. David F. Toal, formerly a student at the Georgia Institute of Technology, prepared most of the computer programs upon which much of this work is based. James N. Duffy, formerly a VISTA volunteer in Atlanta and currently a graduate student at the Louisiana State University in New Orleans, worked with me on the onerous task of classifying urban voting precincts in the face of shifting populations, changing neighborhoods, and varying precinct boundaries.

The analysis of precinct voting patterns involved the dual problem of collecting precinct voter returns and of keeping track of precinct boundary changes. For assistance in these matters, I am deeply indebted to William J. Graham, Jr., Fulton County elections supervisor; James J. Little, Atlanta city clerk; and Veda Terrill, ordinary court clerk for Bibb County.

George Doss, political editor for the Macon *Telegraph*, generously explained to me some of the intricacies of Macon politics and permitted me to examine voter registration data in his possession. Archie N. McKay, city editor for the *Telegraph*, allowed me to make full use of the *Telegraph* library. Professor Hugh D. Graham of the Institute of Southern History, Professor Morris Mitzner of the Georgia Institute of Technology, and Selby McCash, capitol correspondent for the Macon *Telegraph*, read and made helpful comments on the manuscript.

All errors of fact or judgment that have found their way into the following pages are, of course, exclusively my own.

From
Thurmond
to
Wallace

An Introduction

Traditionally, the South has been the nation's most politically unique region. Many factors, of course, have contributed to southern political distinctiveness. Among them have been slavery, defeat in war, the Reconstruction experience, a staple-crop economy, poverty, ruralism, a predominately Anglo-Saxon white population, a Protestant and often fundamentalist religious orientation, de jure racial segregation, a regional mythology that grew out of these experiences, and, most of all, the persistent white concern for the maintenance of white supremacy in the social order. Although the uniqueness of the South's historical background should not be exaggerated, the region has often demonstrated a somewhat deviant political deportment.[1]

---

[1] W. J. Cash, *The Mind of the South* (New York: Alfred A. Knopf, 1941), and C. Vann Woodward, *The Burden of Southern History* (rev. ed.;

During the twentieth century, the predominant manifestations of southern political sectionalism have been the one-party system and disfranchisement. Both of these practices emerged hand-in-hand with enforced segregation, and the basic purpose of both was the promotion and protection of white supremacy. "At the origin of the southern one-party system stood the single figure of the Negro," Professor Alexander Heard has written, and the same observation is equally valid for the disfranchisement movement.[2] In his classic study of southern politics, the late V. O. Key concluded that

southern sectionalism and the special character of southern political institutions have to be attributed in the main to the Negro. The one-party system, suffrage restrictions departing from democratic norms, low levels of voting and of political interest, and all the consequences of these political arrangements and practices must be traced ultimately to this one factor. All of which amounts to saying that the predominant consideration in the architecture of southern political institutions has been to assure locally a subordination of the Negro population, and, externally, to block threatened interferences from the outside with these local arrangements.[3]

Together, the one-party system and disfranchisement not only served in the defense of white supremacy but also tended to stultify southern politics. Key and Heard have described the inadequacy of single-party politics to express clearly and openly even the simplest dialectic. The "southern one- or non-party system," despite significant diversity from state to state, generally tended to encourage voters to favor local candidates in a "friends and neighbors" fashion, to confuse voter comprehension of the relationship between candidates and programs, to eliminate party discipline and party responsibility, to incline campaigns toward contests of personality rather than tests of issues, to promote showmanship in

---

Baton Rouge: Louisiana State University Press, 1968), are perhaps the most important examinations of the significance of the South's historical evolution.

[2] Alexander Heard, *A Two-Party South?* (Chapel Hill: University of North Carolina Press, 1952), p. 9.

[3] V. O. Key, Jr., with the assistance of Alexander Heard, *Southern Politics in State and Nation* (New York: Alfred A. Knopf, 1949), p. 665.

elections and irresponsibility in office, and, in overall effect, to benefit the "haves" of society at the expense of the "have nots."[4]

Negro disfranchisement and low voting levels among the less economically privileged whites sharply narrowed the base of southern politics. More prosperous members of southern white society participated in the democratic process only slightly less frequently than more affluent citizens outside the region. Lower class whites, however, were far less likely than their nonsouthern peers to become actively involved in the political process. In 1956 only 41 percent of southern blue-collar workers voted in the presidential election; 76 percent of nonsouthern workers cast ballots. Heard observed that "the absence from the electorate of large numbers of poor whites, plus the absence of huge numbers of Negroes, weights the electorate in favor of the 'haves.' Politicians would feel more need to cultivate lower income groups if more of them voted."[5] Key similarly speculated that "if the blue-collar vote in the South should double, southern conservatives in Congress would probably become less numerous."[6]

Thus the one-party system and disfranchisement have served as effective barriers to the political expression of the mutual economic interests of poorer whites and Negroes. Disfranchisement and, to a substantial extent, single-party politics grew out of the political struggles of the 1890's, when the Populists sought to create an alliance of the "have nots" across color lines. This projected coalition threatened white supremacy by offering political power to Negroes. The white reaction led to the solidification of the one-party system, disfranchisement, and a precipitous decline in voting generally.[7] Combined with the pervasive influence of white supremacy and growing legislative malapportionment, these institutions contributed greatly to the political triumph of southern conservatism.

[4] Heard, *A Two-Party South?*, pp. 3–19; Key, *Southern Politics*, pp. 298–311. See also Paul Lewinson, *Race, Class, and Party: A History of Negro Suffrage and White Politics in the South* (New York: Grosett and Dunlap, 1932), pp. 185–99.

[5] Heard, *A Two-Party South?*, pp. 12–13.

[6] V. O. Key, Jr., *Public Opinion and American Democracy* (New York: Alfred A. Knopf, 1961), p. 105.

[7] Dewey W. Grantham, Jr., *The Democratic South* (Athens: University of Georgia Press, 1963), pp. 15–41.

By the late 1960's, however, the institutional manifestations of southern distinctiveness were in sharp decline. Urbanization and industrialization had produced a growing Republican party that challenged one-party rule in urban, state, and presidential politics. With the exception of traditionally Republican mountain counties, rural and small town areas remained safe for local Democratic. leaders throughout most of the South. Urban Democrats, however, faced an increasingly formidable Republican opposition, and the G.O.P. recorded impressive victories in state elections. In 1968 Republican governors sat in the state houses of Arkansas and Florida, and Republicans from Florida, South Carolina, Tennessee, and Texas served in the United States Senate. Hubert H. Humphrey finished third in the balloting in five of the eleven former Confederate states and carried only Texas. Similarly, voter participation below the Potomac had increased sharply. By 1968 approximately 78 percent of whites and 62 percent of Negroes of voting age population were registered.[8] Registration and voter turn-out in the South still lagged behind national norms, but the gap was closing. At the same time, United States Supreme Court decisions gave urban representatives in the South, as elsewhere in the nation, an equitable voice in the state legislative process. These events have shifted the institutional foundation of southern politics.

Several studies of southern political trends have offered evidence of a more rational political order emerging from the ruins of the old system. Professor Walter Dean Burham, in his examination of the 1962 senatorial election in Alabama, perceived "strong evidences of critical political realignment" in the South and noted "the similarity of response" displayed by the poorer whites of north Alabama and the Negroes who were safe from white intimidation in the southern part of the state.[9] In Tennessee, Professor Norman L. Parks found "Negroes, labor, urban low-income whites, small farmers, and liberals generally" joining together in the liberal

[8] Voter Education Project, Southern Regional Council, *Voter Registration in the South: Summer, 1968* (Atlanta: Southern Regional Council, 1968), p. 1.

[9] Walter Dean Burnham, "The Alabama Senatorial Election of 1962: Return of Inter-Party Competition," *Journal of Politics* 26 (November, 1964): 800, 817.

wing of the Democratic party.[10] Texas liberal Democratic voting strength was found to rest on ethnic and racial minorities, industrial laborers, and Populist-oriented farmers.[11] Although the influence of Bourbon conservatives remained strong in Democratic parties throughout the South, the Republican party was steadily winning the allegiance of higher-income citizens, especially in the cities. These studies suggested the growth of political alignments broadly pitting the "have nots" against the "haves." in a politics based on class and economic issues.

This work examines voter response to the changing structure of political competition in the state of Georgia. As in other southern states, Georgia's political institutions are passing through a period of sweeping change. The rise of a vigorous, urban-based Republican party, a dramatic increase in voter participation, the destruction of the county unit system and legislative malapportionment, and the re-entry of Negroes into the political arena have combined with continuing urbanization and industrialization to metamorphose the state's political profile.

In 1964 a Republican presidential candidate won Georgia's electoral votes, a feat never before achieved by a nominee of the party of Lincoln. In 1966 the G.O.P. nominee for governor won a plurality of the popular vote. In 1968 the Republican presidential candidate ran ahead of the Democratic contender, although the American Independent party ticket won the state. The Republican appeal in these elections appeared to rest on considerably more than the anger of "mad Democrats" or other transient issues. To be sure, Georgians, like southerners generally, by and large still considered themselves to be Democrats in terms of party identification.[12] Nevertheless, the persistent, if somewhat uneven, gains recorded by Republican candidates on every level of election competition strongly suggested the growing maturity of two-party politics in the state. Table 1-1 records the percentage of Georgia's

[10] Norman L. Parks, "Tennessee Politics Since Kefauver and Reece: A 'Generalist' View," *Journal of Politics* 28 (February, 1966): 161.

[11] James R. Soukup, Clifton McCleskey, and Harry Holloway, *Party and Factional Division in Texas* (Austin: University of Texas Press, 1964), p. 96.

[12] Donald R. Matthews and James W. Prothro, *Negroes and the New Southern Politics* (New York: Harcourt, Brace and World, 1966), pp. 372-77.

popular vote for president received by the Republican party during two decades.

Table 1-1

Percentage of Votes Received by Republican Presidential Candidates, 1948–68

1948	1952	1956	1960	1964	1968
18.3%	30.3%	33.3%	37.4%	54.1%	30.4%

Source: Richard M. Scammon (comp. and ed.), *America at the Polls: A Handbook of American Presidential Election Statistics, 1920–1964* (Pittsburgh: University of Pittsburgh Press, 1965), pp. 105–13; 1968 figure based on returns provided by Secretary of State, Georgia.

As the table indicates, the Republican share of the election returns spurted upward in 1952 and again in 1964. In both 1944 and 1948, the Republican candidate received 18.3 percent of the vote. Voters dissatisfied with the Democratic Fair Deal and civil rights programs found Dwight D. Eisenhower's personal appeal and state's rights philosophy too attractive to resist. General Eisenhower's campaign established the G.O.P. as the party of affluent middle class voters in the cities and suburbs. Barry Goldwater's anti-civil rights position tempted numerous traditionally Democratic voters (as well as many habitual nonvoters) and led large numbers of white Georgians to vote Republican for the first time. Many of these temporary Republican recruits deserted to George C. Wallace in 1968, but the Republicans fared well in the cities and suburbs and won 53.2 percent of the major party vote.[13]

Not until the 1960's did the Republican party offer serious competition in congressional races. In the 1964 election, candidates campaigned under the G.O.P. banner in five of Georgia's ten congressional districts. Capitalizing on Goldwater's popularity in the state, the Republicans won one House seat and made impressive showings in other contests. Congressional Republicanism

[13] These elections are more fully examined in later chapters. For helpful statistics on Republican voting in recent elections, see John C. Topping, Jr., John R. Lazarek, and William H. Linder, *Southern Republicanism and the New South* (Cambridge, Mass.: Republicans for Progress and the Ripon Society, 1966), and Republican National Committee, *The 1968 Elections: A Summary Report with Supporting Tables* (Washington: Republican National Committee, 1969).

reached a peak in 1966 when the G.O.P. fielded eight candidates and elected two House members, both from the Atlanta area. The party retained these two seats in the 1968 election. Table 1-2 shows the percentage of votes won by Republican candidates for the United States House of Representatives between 1948 and 1968.

Table 1-2

Percentage of Votes Received by Republican Congressional Candidates, 1948–68

1948-52	1954	1956	1958	1960	1962	1964	1966	1968
0	8.7	10.2	0	4.3	17.9	30.6	34.4	20.5

Source: Republican National Committee, *The 1968 Elections: A Summary with Supporting Tables* (Washington: Republican National Committee, 1969), p. 115.

A Republican has yet to win a state-level office in Georgia. In 1966 the party polled 46.5 percent of the vote in its first serious effort to capture the Georgia governorship. The Republican senatorial candidate two years later polled a not unrespectable 22.5 percent against incumbent Herman E. Talmadge. In local politics the Grand Old Party has recorded impressive victories in Macon, Savannah, Columbus, and other urban areas, and in 1969 it held 34 of the 251 seats in the state legislature.

While distinctly a minority party, the G.O.P. seems to have established itself as a functional alternative to Democratic rule. The party appears well-financed, and it appeals to a substantial state-wide following. Its organizational machinery, especially in urban areas, is generally more efficient and effective than that possessed by the Democrats. As an institutional foundation of Georgia politics, the one-party system no longer exists.

Growing voter participation provides further evidence of political transition. During the two decades 1940–60, Georgia's population increased by 26.2 percent; during the two decades 1948–68, voter turnout for presidential elections increased by just under 200 percent. Again, caution is in order. Citizen participation in the democratic process in Georgia remained well below the national norm. Table 1-3 shows the percentage of voting age population in Georgia and in the United States that visited the polling booths in the presidential elections of 1960, 1964, and 1968. In the 1968 election, approximately 44 percent of Georgia's voting age population and 68 percent of the state's registered voters cast ballots, whereas 61 percent of the national voting population and 81 percent of the nation's registrants voted.[14]

Table 1-3

Percentage of Voting Age Population Voting in Presidential Elections, 1960–68

Year	Georgia	United States
1960	30.1	63.7
1964	43.2	62.0
1968	44.1	61.0

Source: Republican National Committee, *The 1968 Elections*, p. 15.

The upsurge of popular democracy in Georgia, as Tables 1-3 and 1-4 indicate, occurred before passage of the 1965 voting rights law. Negro voter registration increased most rapidly during the 1962-64 period. To be sure, Negroes had participated actively in Georgia politics since the mid-1940's when federal court decisions struck down the white primary.[15] By the early 1950's, widely varying estimates placed Negro registration somewhere between 60,000 and 145,000.[16] Although confined for the most part to the cities and larger towns, Negro voter registration increased during the 1950's and reached an estimated 180,000 by 1960. This figure represented 15 percent of the total names on the state's voter lists and 29.4 percent of the Negro population of voting age. The number of registered Negro voters declined slightly in the early part of the 1960's, but it increased sharply between 1962 and 1964. By 1964 the number of black registrants had jumped to 270,000, which was 44.1 percent of potential Negro voters. The 1965 voting rights bill had less effect on Negro politi-

[14] Republican National Committee, *The 1968 Elections*, pp. 249-50.

[15] *Smith* v. *Allright*, 321 U.S. 664 (1944); *Chapman* v. *King*, 154 F.2d 460 (1946); Clarence A. Bacote, "The Negro Voter in Georgia Politics, To-day," *Journal of Negro Education* 26 (Summer, 1957): 307–18.

[16] The lower estimate was by Joseph L. Bernd, *Grass Roots Politics in Georgia: The County Unit System and the Importance of the Individual Voting Community in Bi-Factional Elections, 1942-1954* (Atlanta: Emory University, 1960), p. 30; the higher estimate was by Margaret Price, *The Negro and the Ballot in the South* (Atlanta: Southern Regional Council, 1959), p. 9.

cal participation in Georgia than in some other states, and Negro voter registration has lagged behind the South-wide average. In 1968 black registrants totaled 343,695, which represented 56.1 percent of Negro voting age population and comprised 18.4 percent of registered Georgia voters.

Table 1-4

Estimated White and Black Voter Registration in Georgia by Numbers and as Percentage of Voting Age Population, 1960-68

Year	White		Black	
	number	percent	number	percent
1960	1,020,000	56.8	180,000	29.4
1962	1,152,707	64.1	175,573	28.6
1964	1,340,000	74.6	270,000	44.1
1966	1,373,388	76.5	280,212	45.7
1968	1,523,560	84.8	343,695	56.1

Source: All figures are estimates made by the Voter Education Project of the Southern Regional Council. Figures for 1960, 1962, and 1964 are from *VEP NEWS*, April, 1968, p. 3; 1966 figures from Voter Education Project, Southern Regional Council, *Voter Registration in the South: Summer, 1966* (Atlanta: Southern Regional Council, 1966), Georgia-8; 1968 figures from Voter Education Project, Southern Regional Council, *Voter Registration in the South: Summer, 1968* (Atlanta: Southern Regional Council, 1968), p. 1. Estimates of voter registration vary. These figures should be compared with the figures in United States Commission on Civil Rights, *Political Participation: A Study of the Participation by Negroes in the Electoral and Political Processes in 10 Southern States since Passage of the Voting Rights Act of 1965* (Washington: Government Printing Office, 1968), pp. 232-39, and in Pat Watters and Reese Cleghorn, *Climbing Jacob's Ladder: The Arrival of Negroes in Southern Politics* (New York: Harcourt, Brace and World, 1967), Appendix II.

Although Negro voter registration increased significantly during the 1960's, greater numbers of white citizens in Georgia, as elsewhere in the South, visited voter registration offices. The number of Negro registrants almost doubled; however, three times more white than black citizens added their names to the voter rolls. Some 500,000 whites registered during the 1960's; the Negro gain between 1962 and 1968 was approximately 168,000. The greatest growth in white registration took place during the same 1962-64 period in which the most marked Negro advances were recorded.

Figure 1-1 records voter turnout in presidential and gubernatorial contests over a twenty-two-year period. As the chart suggests, voter participation in Georgia has coincided closely with overall political developments and events. The relatively heavy

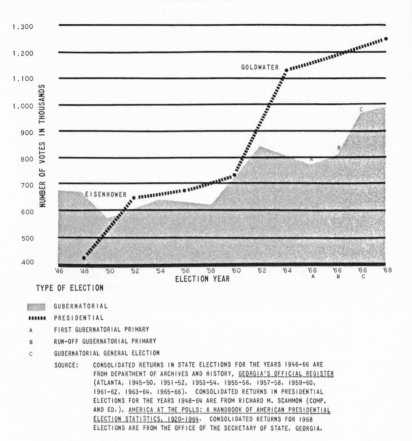

Figure 1-1. Ballots Cast in Gubernatorial and Presidential Elections in Georgia.

voting in the gubernatorial primary elections of 1946 and 1948
reflected the heated factional conflicts within the state Democratic party. The long-standing Democratic monopoly in presidential elections encouraged a popular apathy that even the appearance of the Dixiecrat ticket on the ballots in 1948 was unable
to penetrate. Anti-Negro purges of voter lists in many parts of
Georgia during the late 1940's circumscribed black political participation and tended to offset gains in voter participation attribut-
able to a 1945 liberalization of voter registration requirements.[17]

[17]The 1945 Georgia constitution, while retaining literacy qualifica-
tions, eliminated the poll tax and lowered the voting age to 18; *Constitution*

Although the Eisenhower candidacy in 1952 contributed to an upswing in presidential voting, the deterioration of dual factionalism within the Georgia Democratic party led to a decline in citizen involvement in state political competition during the 1950's. With the coming of the civil rights movement, voting in both national and state elections shot upward in the early 1960's. The first public school desegregation in Georgia, the sit-in movement, freedom rides, civil rights demonstrations, state-federal desegregation clashes at the state universities of Georgia, Alabama, and Mississippi, and the first major national civil rights legislation since Reconstruction affected or seemed to affect the lives of a great many Georgia citizens. Large numbers of whites responded to these developments by going to the polls; the work of the Voter Education Project of the Southern Regional Council during the 1962–64 period combined with the impact of the civil rights movement to augment Negro political participation.[18] Just as the white reaction to the changing place of black people in American life had led to disfranchisement measures and low levels of voting, the shifting position of Negroes motivated substantial numbers of citizens to re-enter the voting booths.

The breakdown of the county unit system and of legislative malapportionment attended the increase in popular democracy and the rise of a two-party system. In 1962 the United States Supreme Court upheld a lower court decision declaring the Georgia county unit system unconstitutional, and during the same year a federal district court ruled that the state general assembly was unconstitutionally apportioned.[19] The state Democratic executive

---

of the State of Georgia, Article II. In 1949 and 1958, the Georgia legislature enacted voter registration laws that included restrictive provisions, but these laws were not widely enforced and had little apparent effect on voter participation. See Joseph L. Bernd and Lynwood M. Holland, "Recent Restrictions upon Negro Suffrage: The Case of Georgia," *Journal of Politics* 21 (August, 1959): 487–513; and Olive H. Shadgett, *Voter Registration in Georgia: A Study of Its Administration* (Athens: University of Georgia Press, 1955).

[18]Matthews and Prothro, *New Southern Politics*, pp. 15–20; Pat Watters and Reese Cleghorn, *Climbing Jacob's Ladder: The Arrival of Negroes in Southern Politics* (New York: Harcourt, Brace and World, 1967), pp. 2–50; Jack Walker, "Negro Voting in Atlanta: 1953–1961," *Phylon* 24 (Winter, 1963): 379–87.

[19]*Sanders* v. *Gray*, 203 F. Supp. 158; *Gray* v. *Sanders*, 372 U.S. 368; *Toombs* v. *Forston*, 205 F. Supp. 248; Ida Martin Chiaraviglis, "The Supreme

committee abandoned the county unit system prior to the 1962 Democratic primaries, and by 1965 the state legislature had formulated a reapportionment plan acceptable to the federal courts. The decisions broke the long-standing rural domination of state politics and offered the opportunity for political practices to adjust to demographic and economic reality.

For more than half a century, the one-party system and a restricted suffrage, buttressed by the county unit system and legislative malapportionment, were the fundamental institutions in Georgia politics. By the late 1960's, these institutions seemed to be in a condition of hopeless disrepair. The re-emergence of the Republican party, increased voter participation, and more democratic institutional arrangements in state politics evidenced the changing political environment.

These developments have not, however, contributed to the emergence of a New Deal politics in the state. V. O. Key and Alexander Heard, writing in the aftermath of the Great Depression, had anticipated that higher voting levels among poorer black and white southerners and a structured two-party rivalry would tend to liberalize politics in the region, and their assumptions have received support from the findings of other scholars. But, in Georgia, these expectations have not been realized. Growing voter registration and two-party competition have failed to give birth to political alignments arraying the "have nots" in opposition to the "haves." The following pages examine the patterns of voter response to the changing institutional foundations of politics in Georgia.

Court, the National Government, and States Rights: An Analysis of Georgia Cases" (Ph.D. dissertation, Emory University, 1962), pp. 186–236; Albert B. Saye, "Revolution by Judicial Action in Georgia," *Western Political Quarterly* 17 (March, 1964): 10–14.

The Politics of the Countryside

Political alignments in Georgia have reflected a variety of conflicting interests. The most pervasive cleavage, as V. O. Key pointed out, has been the dissonance between rural voters and urban voters. In this conflict between city and farm, the larger towns have occupied an important middle position. Townsmen have often tended to identify their interests with their rural neighbors and sometimes with the urban centers that they seek to emulate. Geographical sectionalism has added another element of political discord. The citizens of mountain and piedmont north Georgia, especially those residing in the larger towns, have frequently demonstrated political inclinations that have differed from the positions taken by residents of the south and central Georgia lowlands. Finally, socio-economic divisions based on such factors as income, education, occupation, and race have sundered Georgia political unity. In the cities, as chapter 3 will show, three groups of voters—Negroes, affluent whites, and lower status whites—have viewed political questions from different perspectives.

Historically, rural-urban antagonisms have created the most persistent schism in modern Georgia politics.[1] The "New South" doctrines espoused by Henry W. Grady and his associates appealed primarily to urban areas, and during the post-Reconstruction period, New South politicians governed Georgia in the interest of urban industrial progress. The poorer farmers struck back under the Populist banner in the 1890's. Thomas E. Watson, the most important of the Populist leaders in Georgia, remained in state politics long after the passing of the Populist party, and with ever increasing invectiveness, he rallied rural residents against the cities. After Watson's death, Eugene Talmadge emerged as the defender of rural traditionalism and as the scourge of urban concepts of progress. During recent years the rapid growth of urbanization in Georgia has tended to widen the breach between city and countryside. "Adverse economic and demographic forces," as one scholar has observed in reference to the South generally, "have baffled and frustrated many rural people, exacerbating their fears of social change and their bitter hostility toward the city. Their declining economic and social status has made them more than ever the great conservators of the South's traditions, and they have lost much of the economic radicalism that once made them the cutting edge of southern reform."[2]

The county unit system further aggravated rural-urban dissension. It rewarded the politician who most single-mindedly cultivated the rural vote. The system provided that the candidate in a primary election winning a plurality of the votes in a county carried that county's unit votes. Each county was allotted two unit votes for each member that it elected to the Georgia House of Representatives. All counties chose at least one representative to the lower house of the legislature, and the more populous counties elected either two or three members. Consequently, the 121 least populous counties cast two unit votes each, 30 "middle" counties

[1] Key, *Southern Politics*, pp. 115-19. And see generally C. Vann Woodward, *Tom Watson: Agrarian Rebel* (New York: Oxford University Press, 1938); Alex M. Arnett, *The Populist Movement in Georgia* (New York: Columbia University Press, 1922).

[2] Grantham, *The Democratic South*, p. 88.

possessed four unit votes each, and the eight most populous counties were in the six unit vote category (Table 2-1). This arrangement permitted the least populous counties to dominate both the state legislature and the executive branch of government. The 556,326 people who resided in Fulton County in 1960 cast the same number of unit votes and elected the same number of state representatives as the 6,980 inhabitants of Echols, Glascock, and Quitman Counties.

Table 2-1

County Unit Votes and Population, 1950 and 1960

Number of counties	Unit vote of each county	Total Unit vote	Total population
		—1950—	
8	6	48	1,277,160
30	4	120	907,028
121	2	242	1,310,390
		—1960—	
8	6	48	1,626,734
30	4	120	1,053,530
121	2	242	1,262,852

Source: Louis T. Rigdon II, *Georgia's County Unit System* (Decatur, Ga.: Selective Books, 1961), p. 40.

Rural and small town voters controlled Georgia politics, but these voters did not form an entirely homogeneous group. Broadly, Georgia is divided into three sections: the black belt in the central part of the state, the south, and the hills and mountains to the north. In 1960 approximately 51 percent of the state's people lived in the rural and small town counties that largely comprised these three sections. The other 49 percent of the population resided in 15 urban counties and, before 1962, were effectively disfranchised by malapportionment and the county unit system. The 15 urban counties include all of the state's large cities and major suburban areas. The voting tendencies in Georgia's urban centers will be treated in greater detail in the next chapter. Here the 144 nonurban counties, which possessed the bulk of the county unit votes, are the central concern.[3]

[3] Throughout this work, the term "urban" has been reserved for the large cities and surrounding suburban areas. Smaller cities are referred to as

The black belt encompasses the southwestern part of the state and arches through its center. As defined here, the black belt includes those 54 counties containing a nonwhite population of 40 percent or more. In 1960 something more than 600,000 people, 15.4 percent of the total population of the state, resided in these 54 counties.[4] A majority of the population, 52.5 percent, was nonwhite. Approximately 75 percent of the black belt's people lived outside the limits of towns of 2,500 or more. Although encompassing over 15 percent of Georgia's population, this section received only 10.4 percent of the state's total personal income. The average per capita income in 1960 was under $1,100, well below the state average per capita income of $1,609, and less than half the national per capita average income. The black belt was the poorest and most rural part of Georgia, and substantial numbers of its inhabitants were abandoning the area in search of greener pastures. All but 12 of the section's 54 counties lost population between 1950 and 1960, the average county losing 6.8 percent of its citizens during the decade. In addition to its poverty, the area also contained the largest farms in the state. On the average, a black belt farm was almost 100 acres larger than a typical Georgia farm. Overall, the Georgia black belt differed little from black belt areas of other southern states. It was a predominately rural section peopled by substantial white land owners and wretched masses, the majority of whom were black and a considerable number of whom were fleeing to other areas.

To the south and east of the black belt is a region of smaller farms and higher relative white population. The historical evolu-

---

"towns" (see Figure 2-3). The precise dividing line between "city" and "town" is explained in chapter 3. On the functioning of the county unit system, see Louis T. Rigdon II, *Georgia's County Unit System* (Decatur, Ga.: Selective Books, 1961); Cullen B. Gosnell, "Small Counties Rule: Georgia's Method of Apportionment for Legislature Places Control of State in Hands of Rural Areas," *National Municipal Review* 47 (July, 1958): 332-34; and William G. Cornelius, "The County Unit System of Georgia: Facts and Prospects," *Western Political Quarterly* 14 (December, 1961): 942-60.

[4] Statistics in the discussion are based on Bureau of Business and Economic Research, Graduate School of Business Administration, University of Georgia, *Georgia: Statistical Abstract 1968* (Athens: University of Georgia Press, 1968), and U. S. Bureau of the Census, *U.S. Census of Population: 1960*, vol. I, *Characteristics of the Population*, pt. 12, *Georgia* (Washington: Government Printing Office, 1963).

tion of this section differed from that of the black belt. When the whites of the black belt took up arms in the 1860's to defend their flourishing Old South civilization, the southern portion of the state was still heavily timbered and sparsely populated. In 1960 the 43 rural and small town counties in this region contained a population of approximately 550,000, 13.8 percent of the population of the state. About 70 percent of these people were white, and approximately 64 percent were rural. The area received less than 10 percent of the state's total personal income, and the average per capita income of something over $1,100 was only 70 percent of the state average. The farms in this region were significantly smaller than those in the black belt but were somewhat larger than the average farm in the state. Thirty of the 43 counties in this section lost population during the 1950–60 period. In a typical county, 4.7 percent of the people departed for other places during the decade. This region resembled the black belt more closely than it did the northern part of Georgia. As Figure 2–1 shows, the two sections geographically overlapped. Several counties located within the general area of the black belt contained a black population of less than 40 percent and were classified as non-black-belt south; several counties in the southeastern part of the state embraced a nonwhite population greater than 40 percent and were placed in the black belt category. The southeastern portion of Georgia was second only to the black belt in the extent of its poverty; it was predominately rural; its population was declining; and it shared kinship ties with the black belt.

Northern Georgia differed significantly from the southern part of the state. Traditionally a land of small farmers, north Georgia, like the upland regions of other southern states, produced a disproportionate share of "Scalawags" during Reconstruction and Populists during the agrarian upheavals of the 1890's. More recently, new industries have located in this section far more frequently than in other nonurban areas, and a relatively high percentage of the work force labored in manufacturing.[5] Although

[5] Ray M. Northam, *Factors Influencing Recent Industrial Growth in Northeastern Georgia* (Athens: Institute of Community and Area Development, 1962); John C. Belcher, *The Dynamics of Georgia's Population* (Athens: University of Georgia Press, 1964); pp. 4–6; John C. Meadows, *Modern Georgia* (rev. ed.; Athens: University of Georgia Press, 1954), pp. 285–96.

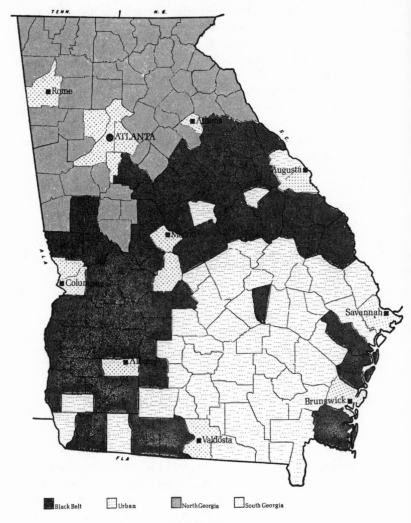

Figure 2-1.

much of this manufacturing growth was in "soft," exploitive industries, the factory payrolls contributed to a per capita income substantially higher than that enjoyed by south Georgians. The approximately 860,000 people residing in north Georgia made up 21.8 percent of the state's population and received 18.4 percent of its total personal income. The average per capita income of almost

$1,400 was 86 percent of the state average. A majority of north Georgia's 47 counties gained population during the 1950-60 period. The population was over 85 percent white in 1960, and some 70 percent was rural. A typical farm in this region was substantially smaller than the Georgia average.

In the 1968 presidential election, the 144 nonurban counties cast 51 percent of the popular vote. Twenty years before, these counties had returned almost 60 percent of the total ballots in the presidential election and more than 65 percent in the gubernatorial contest. Figure 2-2 records each section's percentage of the popular vote in major elections during the 1948-68 period. The county unit system presumably accounted, in part at least, for the tendency of rural and small town residents in south and central Georgia to demonstrate significantly greater interest in gubernatorial primary elections than in presidential contests. Despite the disfranchisement of black voters in many rural areas of the state during most of this period, rural and small town voters still participated in elections relatively more often than urban-suburban voters. In 1960 the three nonurban sections contained 51 percent of the population and cast 54.2 percent of the popular vote for president.

A majority of the people living in the nonurban portions of south Georgia, the central black belt, and north Georgia dwelled in a rural-village environment; however, a consequential number resided in the larger towns. The county unit system, while it effectively disfranchised the cities, did in some aspects enhance the influence of the towns throughout the state. Any candidate in a primary election who felt rural voters might favor the opposition had of necessity to pursue the votes of townsmen.[6] In addition to sectional and socio-economic class factors, county unit politics revolved around a diluted urban vote, a magnified rural vote, and an important town vote.

Excluding the cities and suburban communities, 29 Georgia counties contained substantial towns. Fourteen of these counties included towns of above 10,000 population in 1960. Fourteen other counties contained a town of 7,000 and a population more

---

[6]This point is admirably developed in Bernd, *Grass Roots Politics*, pp. 21-28.

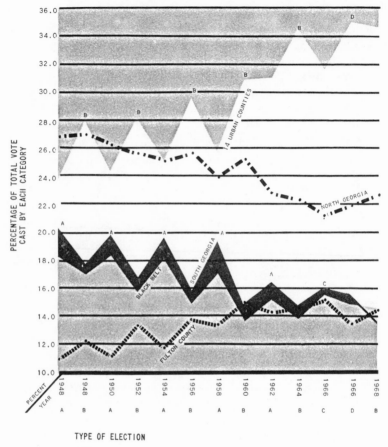

TYPE OF ELECTION

A   PRIMARY FOR GOVERNOR
B   ELECTION OF PRESIDENT
C   RUN-OFF PRIMARY FOR GOVERNOR
D   GENERAL ELECTION FOR GOVERNOR

Figure 2-2. Percentage of Votes Cast in Gubernatorial and Presidential Elections.

than 30 percent urban, or a town of above 6,000 and a population more than 40 percent urban.[7] Additionally, Walker County, located within the Chattanooga, Tennessee, metropolitan statistical area, encompassed two relatively significant communities of some

[7] All nonurban counties containing a town of more than 6,000 were classified as "town counties," except Walton County, a predominately rural county containing a county seat town (Monroe) of above 6,000.

5,000 people each and was included as the twenty-ninth county in this category. The black belt contained five counties in which townsmen formed a major part of the voting population; south Georgia counted 11; and north Georgia, 13 (Figure 2-3). Table 2-2 shows the population distribution among the predominately rural counties and the counties containing larger towns.

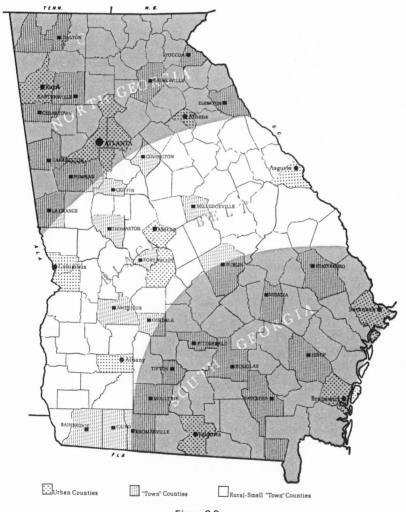

Figure 2-3.

21

Table 2-2

Rural Counties and "Town" Counties (1960 Population)

Section	Rural Counties		"Town" Cos.		Total Cos.	
	no.	pop.	no.	pop.	no.	pop.
South Georgia	32	274,951	11	270,753	43	545,704
Black Belt	49	492,486	5	115,788	54	608,274
North Georgia	34	435,821	13	422,356	47	858,177
Total	115	1,203,258	29	808,897	144	2,012,155

Politically, the townsmen of south and central Georgia and rural voters throughout the state have been Georgia's most conservative voters. Progressivism has resided in the cities and suburbs and in the larger towns in the northern hill county. The complex and multi-dimensional terms "conservative" and "progressive" will be more fully defined in later chapters. Here, the words are used simply to describe voter behavior within the context of Georgia state politics. Conservatives consistently supported the protection and promotion of the county unit system in politics and white supremacy in the social order. They favored the Talmadge faction in state Democratic party conflicts. Progressive voters tended to cast their ballots in opposition to the county unit system, the candidates of the Talmadge faction, and the more extreme white supremacy measures.

Three elections between 1952 and 1960 seemed to offer voters relatively clear choices between basic social and political alternatives. In 1952 Georgians voted on a constitutional amendment that (had it passed) would have expanded and constitutionally formalized the county unit system. The amendment was blatantly antidemocratic, and proponents of the measure assured voters that the county unit system was a bulwark of segregation. While rural voters could have been expected to favor the amendment out of self-interest and urban voters to oppose it for the same reason, the election did clearly structure a crucial issue in Georgia politics.

The Talmadge faction, led by Herman E. Talmadge after his father's death in 1946, sponsored and strongly supported the unsuccessful county unit amendment measure. Two years later the Talmadge forces were back in the field with a constitutional amendment that permitted private schools to be substituted for the public school system. This antidesegregation device posed a direct threat to public education in the state, and thus the election offered voters an opportunity to establish a public policy concerning the relative importance of white supremacy and public education. The amendment passed.[8] In 1960 the Georgia Democratic party conducted a referendum to determine if the state's Democratic presidential electors should be "pledged" to the national party ticket or remain "free" to vote as they would. The meaning of the terms "free" and "pledged" no doubt confused some voters, but the election nevertheless structured a division between the more nationally oriented citizens and the uncompromising defenders of the "southern way of life."[9] Table 2-3 records the results of these three popular elections. The numbers indicate the percentages of voters in the various categories who took "conservative" positions and favored the county unit amendment, the private school amendment, and "free" electors.

Table 2-3

Percentage of Conservative Votes in Three Selected Elections

Election	South Total (rural) (town)	Black Belt Total (rural) (town)	North Total (rural) (town)	14 Urban Cos.	Fulton County (Atl.)
For County Unit–1952	67.5 (74.8) (58.5)	61.4 (64.1) (49.6)	47.9 (54.1) (40.5)	35.8	29.4
For Private School Plan–1954	68.2 (73.4) (61.5)	64.7 (66.4) (57.8)	54.1 (55.8) (52.0)	44.2	41.8
For "Free" Electors–1960	64.8 (62.5) (67.2)	61.2 (60.5) (64.2)	51.9 (49.7) (54.1)	56.4	43.7

Conservatism, at least in relation to the county unit system, public school segregation, and political independence, tended to reside in the rural and southern portions of the state. A simple average of the percentages listed in Table 2-3 gives rural south Georgia a 70.2 percent conservative average vote; the rural black

[8] Rigdon, *Georgia's County Unit System*, pp. 32–41; Bernd, *Grass Roots Politics*, pp. 15–20; Numan V. Bartley, *The Rise of Massive Resistance: Race and Politics in the South during the 1950's* (Baton Rouge: Louisiana State University Press, 1969), pp. 54–55.

[9] Atlanta *Constitution*, September 7, 8, 14, and 15, 1960.

belt, 63.7; south Georgia town counties, 62.3; black belt town counties, 57.2; and rural north Georgia, 53.2. Urban voters and north Georgia townsmen tended to oppose antiprogressive measures. The average vote for the conservative position in north Georgia counties containing larger towns was 48.9 percent; in Fulton County, 38.3; and in the other principal urban counties, 45.5. Rural voters throughout the state indicated greater devotion to the county unit system and less regard for public education than did neighboring townsmen. The greater town and city support for "free" electors may have been in part the result of voter confusion over the issues involved.[10]

The Talmadge faction of the Georgia Democratic party consistently offered the most conservative—more correctly in many cases the most reactionary—social, ideological, and economic programs and policies available to Georgia voters. Not surprisingly, the same citizens who endorsed the county unit system, placed white supremacy above public education, and favored "free" electors also tended to support the Talmadge faction. Anti-Talmadge candidates fared well in the cities and the north Georgia towns; the south and central lowlands and the rural counties in the northern hills were the heartland of Talmadgism. The voters who favored the Talmadge candidates did not, of course, necessarily endorse all of that faction's programs. Both Eugene and Herman Talmadge were excellent campaigners, and each projected a (white) common man, "hell-of-a-fellow" image. "Ol' Gene," for example, pastured a cow on the lawn of the governor's mansion. "Mrs. Talmadge did not like the milk which was being delivered at the Mansion," Talmadge's biographer explained, "so she had Bossy brought up from the farm to browse about on the lawn and to supply the family with rich milk and butter."[11] However great Mrs. Talmadge's fondness for fresh milk and butter, the presence of the bovine beast no doubt enhanced the governor's image among the residents of the countryside. Herman Talmadge, recognizing that demographic changes were taking place in the state,

---

[10] In the city of Macon, Negroes voted for "free" electors, in part, apparently, because of a misinterpretation of the meaning of the word "free."

[11] Allen Lumpkin Henson, *Red Galluses: A Story of Georgia Politics* (Boston: House of Edinboro, 1945), p. 267.

made overtures to city voters and ultimately won a substantial urban following while retaining the allegiance of rural dwellers. In national politics the successive leaders of the Talmadge faction did battle with the New Deal, the Fair Deal, President Truman's civil rights program, the 1954 school desegregation decision, and other reform movements. The state-level policies championed by the two Talmadges differed, although the programs of both men were solidly conservative.[12]

Eugene Talmadge conducted the last of his many primary election campaigns in 1946. In his quest for the governorship, Talmadge stressed the racial issue, promising to restore the white primary and to counter the "Communistic doctrines from outside the state" that were disrupting racial harmony.[13] Talmadge's strongest opponent was James V. Carmichael, an Atlanta area lawyer and businessman. A third major candidate, however, divided the anti-Talmadge vote. Carmichael, with the support of outgoing Governor Ellis G. Arnall, won a plurality of the popular returns, but Talmadge's rural appeal and superior organization carried the county unit vote and gave him the victory. Talmadge easily won the general election in November, 1946, but he died shortly before his inauguration. The Georgia constitution was unclear on who should become governor in this eventuality, and the famous "two governors" controversy ensued. The state legislature chose as governor Herman Talmadge, who had received a sufficient number of write-in votes to finish second in the general election. When Governor Arnall refused to surrender the office, Talmadge, with the aid of supporters and units of the state police and the

---

[12] On the Talmadge faction in Georgia politics, see *ibid.*; Key, *Southern Politics*, pp. 106–29; Sarah McCulloh Lemmon, "The Ideology of Eugene Talmadge," *Georgia Historical Quarterly* 38 (September, 1954): 226–48; Bernd, *Grass Roots Politics*, pp. 6–36; and Bartley, *Rise of Massive Resistance*, pp. 40–43, 68–70. Generally speaking, the leaders of the anti-Talmadge faction were not "liberals," if that term is defined to include open support for such things as racial integration and labor unions. Nevertheless, the anti-Talmadge faction stood far to the left of the Talmadgites. Something of the flavor of the differing outlooks of the two factions can be obtained by comparing Ellis Gibbs Arnall, *The Shore Dimly Seen* (New York: J. B. Lippincott Co., 1946), and Herman E. Talmadge, *You and Segregation* (Birmingham: Vulcan, 1955).

[13] As quoted in the Macon *News*, July 18, 1946.

national guard, seized control of the state capitol and the governor's mansion. After a brief period as governor-in-exile, Arnall abdicated his claim to the office in favor of incoming Lieutenant Governor Melvin E. Thompson, who took the oaths for both lieutenant governor and governor. At this point, Thompson and Talmadge each claimed the governorship, with the latter occupying the executive department. Eventually, the state supreme court awarded the office to Thompson.[14]

The issue was ultimately settled in the 1948 special gubernatorial primary election. Herman Talmadge carried his faction's banner; Thompson was the candidate of the anti-Talmadge forces. In the campaign, Talmadge championed white supremacy and attacked Thompson's record as acting governor. The voters awarded Talmadge a majority of both the popular and county unit votes. By 1950 the Talmadge administration faced serious financial problems, and the anti-Talmadge forces, again led by M. E. Thompson, offered a formidable challenge in the 1950 Democratic primary for governor. The Talmadge faction's organizational superiority contributed substantially to Talmadge's re-election. He won a majority of the county unit votes and a narrow plurality of the popular ballots.

Two factors greatly strengthened the Talmadge faction's position during the early 1950's. Unlike his father, Herman Talmadge possessed a sense of urban and industrial progress, and he proved to be a capable executive and administrator. His administration successfully sponsored legislation increasing consumer taxes, expanding state services, and defending racial segregation. His record as governor and his personal appeal contributed to his growing popularity in the state. Second, the *Brown* v. *Board of Education* decision, in which the United States Supreme Court declared de jure school segregation unconstitutional, politically benefited the Talmadge faction. Long recognized as unwavering defenders of white supremacy, the Talmadge forces now had an immediate threat to resist. By the time of the 1954 gubernatorial primary campaign, the governor's prestige and the backlash caused by the *Brown* decision made the Talmadge faction's candidate an almost

[14] This episode is lucidly reviewed by Charles Moore in the Atlanta *Constitution*, November 21, 1966.

certain winner. With Talmadge constitutionally ineligible for re-election, a number of the Talmadge lieutenants made known their availability. Ultimately, three candidates—S. Marvin Griffin, Tom Linder, and Fred Hand—emerged from the Talmadge camp. During the campaign,' Hand won the endorsement of the Atlanta daily newspapers and became something of a "best element" candidate. Therefore, Lieutenant Governor Griffin and Commissioner of Agriculture Linder most clearly represented the Talmadge position. M. E. Thompson and state legislator Charles Gowen were the leading anti-Talmadge contenders.

Griffin reaped the benefits of Talmadge's governorship. With unofficial support from the governor himself, Griffin won a plurality of the popular vote and almost 75 percent of the county unit ballots. Having failed to win despite the three-way split in the opposition camp, a number of disappointed anti-Talmadge leaders, including former Governor Ellis Arnall, surrendered the field and retired to private life. Thompson made one more effort by opposing Talmadge for a seat in the United States Senate in 1956, and his dismal showing confirmed that anti-Talmadgism was dead. So, however, was Talmadgism. The 1954 schism, Talmadge's absence from state politics, and the lack of a coherent opposition made that faction little more than an amorphous group of political leaders. Georgia politics during the late 1950's and early 1960's might have been described as an "era of good feelings." Talmadge won more than 80 percent of the popular vote in his 1956 senatorial victory, and S. Ernest Vandiver, a friend to Talmadge, a relative to Senator Richard B. Russell, and the choice of most of the state's major politicians, received more than 80 percent of the popular ballots in the 1958 gubernatorial primary. The conflict between New South progressivism and rural traditionalism was only submerged, however. When Marvin Griffin sought to return to the governor's office by challenging Carl E. Sanders of Augusta in the 1962 primary, the Talmadge and anti-Talmadge voting patterns reappeared.

As Table 2–4 indicates, the Talmadge faction appealed to the same blocs of voters with considerable consistency. Indeed, the stability of the Talmadge voter coalition was greater than might have been expected. The county unit system, as Professor Joseph L. Bernd has demonstrated, encouraged the formation of county

Table 2-4

Percentage of Votes Received by Talmadge Candidates, 1946-62

Election and Candidate	South total (rural) (town)	Black Belt total (rural) (town)	North total (rural) (town)	14 urban cos.	Fulton Co. (Atl.)
Talmadge 1946 Primary	52.5 (55.5) (48.8)	52.3 (52.8) (49.7)	42.5 (46.8) (37.2)	38.2	24.9
Talmadge 1948 Primary	60.8 (62.8) (58.0)	58.6 (59.3) (55.1)	52.2 (55.7) (47.3)	46.2	34.0
Talmadge 1950 Primary	56.6 (59.9) (52.6)	55.0 (56.5) (47.8)	49.7 (53.3) (45.0)	46.2	32.6
Griffin-Linder 1954 Primary	60.5 (62.8) (57.3)	55.9 (56.2) (54.5)	55.8 (59.1) (51.7)	39.9	31.3
Griffin 1962 Primary	51.0 (54.9) (46.1)	54.4 (54.2) (55.8)	40.7 (44.5) (36.0)	31.7	22.1

political machines and, in some cases, outright graft in the counting and reporting of election results.[15] It also created a "bandwagon" effect by frequently rewarding those county leaders whose counties cast unit votes for the winning candidates. Nevertheless, despite occasional fraudulent vote counts and the maneuverings of county leaders, the voters showed a basic persistency in their choice of candidates. Table 2-5 records the coefficients of correlation between Talmadge candidates, including the 1962

Table 2-5

Talmadge Faction Candidate-to-Candidate Correlations, 1946-62

	Eugene Talmadge, 1946	Herman Talmadge, 1948	Herman Talmadge, 1950	Griffin-Linder, 1954	Griffin, 1962
Talmadge, 1946	——	.9903	.9516	.9138	.9645
Talmadge, 1948	.9903	——	.9715	.9480	.9338
Talmadge, 1950	.9516	.9715	——	.9069	.8503
Griffin-Linder, 1954	.9138	.9480	.9069	——	.8816
Griffin, 1962	.9645	.9338	.8503	.8816	——

Correlations are product moment correlations based on eight categories of voters: south Georgia town, south Georgia rural, black belt town, black belt rural, north Georgia town, north Georgia rural, Atlanta, other urban.

[15] Bernd, *Grass Roots Politics*, pp. 36-47.

Table 2-6

Correlations between the Vote for Talmadge Faction Candidates and the Conservative
Vote in Selected Elections, 1946-62

	Pro County Unit Amendment	Pro Private School Amendment	Pro "Free" Electors
Eugene Talmadge 1946 gubernatorial	.9277	.9163	.7867
Herman Talmadge 1948 gubernatorial	.9402	.9228	.7709
Herman Talmadge 1950 gubernatorial	.9335	.8943	.6713
Griffin-Linder 1954 gubernatorial	.8878	.8846	.6436
Griffin 1962 gubernatorial	.8709	.8938	.7689

Griffin vote. Table 2-6 compares the correlations of the votes for the Talmadge faction and the votes in favor of the county unit amendment, the private school plan, and "free" Democratic party electors.[16]

Citizens of south and central Georgia and the rural areas of north Georgia evidenced enthusiasm for the county unit system, segregated schools, "free" electors, and the candidates associated

[16] For the benefit of nonprofessional readers, product moment correlations are mathematical models that determine the degree of association between given variables (in this case, the response of voter categories toward election alternatives). Effectively, the coefficient of correlation between two candidates reduces a scatter-diagram comparing the votes won by each candidate in each voting category to a number. Such measurements, when based upon broad groupings of voters (as is the case here), are relatively crude. See Hayward R. Alker, Jr., *Mathematics and Politics* (New York: Macmillan, 1965), pp. 54-106, and Hubert M. Blalock, Jr., *Social Statistics* (New York: McGraw-Hill, 1960), pp. 273-301. Nevertheless, product moment correlations offer a convenient (and, for the purposes of this study, an adequate) method for comparing the similarity or dissimilarity of the behavior at the polls of voter categories in terms of given candidates. Thus, as Table 2-5 shows, the coefficient of correlation between the vote for Eugene Talmadge in 1946 and the vote for Herman Talmadge in 1948 is a very high .9903, which indicates that the same voting groups offering relatively high support to one candidate also provided relatively strong support for the other (or, put another way, that there was a high degree of relationship between voter behavior toward the two candidates).

with the Talmadge faction. In the eight elections analyzed in Tables 2-3, 2-4, 2-5, and 2-6, the rural areas of south and central Georgia voted conservatively on every occasion; the south Georgia counties containing larger towns took a conservative stance in six of the eight elections; and the black belt town counties and the north Georgia rural counties voted conservatively on five of eight opportunities. (Atlanta voters rejected the conservative position in every election; the other urban counties took an anticonservative position in seven of the eight contests; and the north Georgia counties containing larger towns rejected the conservative alternative on the ballot in five of the eight elections.)

The voter groups demonstrating the most conservative inclinations at the polls in state elections were the Democratic party's most devoted adherents in national politics. The urbane and racially liberal Adlai E. Stevenson, and the equally urbane and racially liberal—and also Catholic—John F. Kennedy, ran best among voters who evidenced the strongest concern for white supremacy, the least interest in democracy and public education, and the greatest support for those gubernatorial candidates who most uninhibitedly vowed to thwart the liberal policies of the national Democratic party.

The votes cast by voter groups for the Democratic party presidential candidate in three elections are recorded in Table 2-7. As the table shows, rural south and central Georgians, the state's most conservative voters, consistently rendered liberal Democratic candidates three-fourths of their votes. Other rural and town counties did almost as well. That the national Democrats ran somewhat

Table 2-7

Percentage of Votes Received by Democratic Presidential Candidates

Candidate	South Total (rural) (town)	Black Belt Total (rural) (town)	North Total (rural) (town)	14 Urban Cos.	Fulton County (Atl.)
Stevenson, 1952	77.6 (79.5) (75.2)	77.2 (78.9) (69.1)	75.4 (73.6) (77.4)	60.2	59.8
Stevenson, 1956	79.6 (81.7) (77.1)	77.1 (78.4) (71.6)	68.5 (67.1) (70.3)	57.5	56.8
Kennedy, 1960	72.7 (74.2) (71.0)	73.5 (74.8) (67.7)	68.8 (68.8) (68.7)	53.2	50.8

better in the town counties of north Georgia than in the rural counties results from the fact that several rural north Georgia mountain counties, because of events that transpired during the Civil War-Reconstruction period, habitually voted Republican.

Table 2-8 shows the correlation coefficients between the vote for Stevenson and Kennedy and the conservative vote in eight state elections. Kennedy's Catholicism apparently failed to substantially disturb the faith of rural and small town citizens in the Democratic party. Professor Charles B. Pyles, after correlating

Table 2-8

Correlations between the Vote for Democratic Presidential Candidates and the Conservative Vote in Selected Elections, 1946-62

	Stevenson, 1952	Stevenson, 1956	Kennedy, 1960
Talmadge, 1946	.7383	.8711	.8652
Talmadge, 1948	.7927	.8910	.8959
Talmadge, 1950	.7817	.8344	.8474
Griffin–Linder, 1954	.8853	.8886	.9498
Pro County Unit, 1952	.8147	.9187	.8758
Pro Private School Plan, 1954	.8532	.9638	.9086
Pro "Free" Electors, 1960	.5006	.7522	.6353
Griffin, 1962	.7213	.8683	.8681

county-level church membership, membership in the Baptist Church, and voting returns in the 1960 election, concluded that "the religious issue was relatively unimportant in Georgia."[17] In 1952 Stevenson's opponent, General Dwight D. Eisenhower, was the beneficiary of some votes cast by "mad Democrats" in rural and small town areas who were upset with Harry Truman's civil rights policies.[18] Consequently, the correlations for Stevenson's 1952 vote are somewhat lower than those for the Democratic tally in 1956 and 1960. Support for "free" electors in the 1960 state Democratic party referendum was relatively stronger in the towns and cities than was the more rurally oriented backing received by

[17] Charles B. Pyles, "Race and Ruralism in Georgia Elections, 1948–1966" (Ph.D. dissertation, University of Georgia, 1967), p. 147.

[18] Donald S. Strong, "The Presidential Election in the South, 1952," *Journal of Politics* 17 (August, 1955): 343–89.

the national Democrats. Generally, however, the correlations between the vote for liberal candidates in national elections and conservative policies on the state level is quite high.

Even the appearance of the States' Rights Democrats in 1948 did little to shake conservative Georgia's attachment to Democratic voting traditions. The Dixiecrats' candidates and segregationist platform lured little better than 20 percent of Georgia's voters. The Dixiecrats appealed to the racial fears and prejudices of white citizens, and the vote for J. Strom Thurmond did perhaps identify the hard-core racist vote in the state.[19] The vote in the 1958 Georgia gubernatorial primary supports this supposition. Ernest Vandiver, who won more than 80 percent of the popular vote, was profoundly conservative. Yet he appeared almost moderate in comparison to his principal opponent, William T. Bodenhamer, a Baptist minister and the former executive secretary of a white supremacy organization called the Georgia States' Rights Council. Bodenhamer's campaign was blisteringly racist even by Georgia standards.[20] The votes for Thurmond and Bodenhamer are recorded in Table 2-9.

Table 2-9

Percentage of Votes Received by Thurmond and Bodenhamer, 1948 and 1958

Candidate	South Total (rural) (town)	Black Belt Total (rural) (town)	North Total (rural) (town)	14 Urban Cos.	Fulton Co. (Atl.)
Thurmond, 1948	24.6 (26.8) (21.9)	29.8 (28.9) (34.0)	10.4 (10.0) (10.9)	26.1	11.9
Bodenhamer, 1958	23.7 (21.4) (26.7)	21.6 (19.9) (30.0)	7.8 (7.7) (8.3)	12.1	5.8

Not too much should be inferred from these two elections. Bodenhamer resided in a south Georgia town county and a "friends and neighbors" vote undoubtedly had some influence on the election. Thurmond received votes from significant numbers of "mad Democrats" who could not bring themselves to cast ballots

---

[19] See Key, *Southern Politics*, pp. 317-44, and Heard, *A Two-Party South?*, pp. 251-79.

[20] *Southern School News*, September and October, 1958.

for the Republican party. Nevertheless, the returns suggested that somewhere around 25 percent of the voters in south and central Georgia placed white supremacy absolutely paramount in their scale of values. The returns also suggested that a purely racist appeal was an inadequate enticement in predominately white north Georgia.

The tendency for Georgia's most conservative voters in state politics to be the most liberal voters in national politics was a political absurdity that could not forever endure. This alignment was rational only so long as the federal government remained aloof from social policy. Then the poorer areas of the state could vote for economic liberalism on the national level and opt for rural-southern-small-town values in state elections. But President Truman's civil rights program created a paradox for tradition-oriented voters who were accustomed to the social values of a caste system and who had been born into the Democratic party, itself, as Professor Jasper B. Shannon has written, "a tradition which symbolizes a long-since outgrown past whose perpetuation is a part of a creed of loyalty to one's forebears. . . ."[21] This same paradox influenced the voting patterns in urban politics.

[21] Jasper Berry Shannon, *Toward a New Politics in the South* (Knoxville: University of Tennessee Press, 1949), pp. 14–15.

The Politics of the City

The residents of the countryside have traditionally determined Georgia's political fate, but the cities have increasingly dominated the state's economic life. By 1960 urban-suburban areas contained 49 percent of Georgia's people and absorbed 61.7 percent of the state's total personal income. Now emancipated from the county unit system and legislative malapportionment, voters in these 15 counties have become crucial to the course of Georgia politics.

Easily the most populous and the most urban of Georgia's counties is Fulton. It contains most of the city of Atlanta, by far the largest city in the state; all of the city of East Point, the state's seventh largest city in 1960; and part of College Park, a city of above 20,000 population. The approximately 556,000 people residing in Fulton County in 1960 made up 14.1 percent of Georgia's total population. More people thus lived in Fulton than resided in the 43 counties of south Georgia. In the 1968 presidential election, Fulton cast 14.4 percent of the state's total popular vote, which was greater than that cast by south Georgia and only slightly less than that cast by the 54 counties of the central Georgia black belt. Although containing 14.1 percent of the state's population, Fulton County received 21.2 percent of Georgia's total personal income. The county's average per capita income of $2,455 was well above the state average of $1,609. Amost 35 percent of the population in 1960 was nonwhite.

Fourteen other urban counties contained 34.9 percent of Georgia's population and absorbed 40.5 percent of its total personal income. Ten of these counties contained cities with 1960 populations of more than 25,000. These counties were Bibb (Macon), Chatham (Savannah), Clarke (Athens), Cobb (Marietta), DeKalb (part of Atlanta), Dougherty (Albany), Floyd (Rome), Lowndes (Valdosta), Muscogee (Columbus), and Richmond (Augusta). The four additional counties classified as urban were Glynn, which contains the coastal city of Brunswick; Clayton, a suburb of Atlanta; Houston, located adjacent to the city of Macon and the home of the city of Warner Robins and the massive Warner Robins Air Force base; and Chattahoochee, located adjacent to the city of Columbus and dominated by the vast Fort Benning military installation.[1] The average per capita income of citizens residing in these 14 counties was slightly above $1,900 in 1960, and all 14 gained population during the 1950–60 decade. Over three-fourths of the population was white. In the 1968 presidential election, the 14 urban–suburban counties cast 34.6 percent of the popular vote.

---

[1] As defined here, the term "urban" encompassed (1) any county containing a city of more than 25,000 population, and (2) any county located adjacent to a major city or containing a city of 20,000 to 25,000 that additionally (a) had 45 percent or more of its adult population composed of high school graduates and (b) possessed an average annual per capita income of above $1,550 in 1960. This definition placed three counties containing communities of above 20,000 population in the "town" category. They were Spalding County (Griffin), Troup County (LaGrange), and Ware County (Waycross). Statistics are based on Bureau of Business and Economic Research, *Georgia: Statistical Abstract 1968*, and U.S. Bureau of the Census, *U.S. Census of the Population: 1960, Georgia*.

Together Fulton and the other large countries were the most prosperous and the most rapidly growing areas of Georgia. They also contained the most progressive voters in the state. It would be erroneous, however, to generalize too freely about the "urban vote." Class and racial divisions split city voters into three fairly distinct groupings, not all of which were oriented toward a politics of progressivism.

To test the voting behavior of urban dwellers, Atlanta and Macon were selected for detailed precinct analysis in this study. Atlanta is the largest and probably the most politically sophisticated city in the state. It has long been an incubator for New South concepts of urban industrial progress. Macon seems to represent a more "typical" Georgia urban community. It is an Old South city resting in the geographical center of the state and partially surrounded by black belt plantation counties. Macon's approximately 70,000 citizens made it the state's fifth largest city in 1960.

In both cities all classifiable voting precincts have been placed in previously defined socio-economic categories.[2] These categories are:

1. Poor White. A majority of the people in this category had less than an eighth grade education, and a majority of the families lived on marginal incomes. The bulk of employed males worked in

---

[2] The model for sorting neighborhoods into socio-economic categories was derived from Community Council of the Atlanta Area, Inc., *Atlanta's People: A Study of Selected Demographic Characteristics of the Population in the Atlanta Metropolitan Area, by Census Tracts, 1960* (Atlanta: Community Council, 1964). That work divided the 1960 census tracts of the five county Atlanta Metropolitan Area into quintiles. The Community Council created a socio-economic index based on the percentage of adults having an eighth grade education or less, the percentage of families receiving incomes of $5,000 or less, and the percentage of males laboring in blue collar occupations. The five counties dealt with by the Community Council contained about 25 percent of Georgia's people, and thus the socio-economic index was based on a substantial sample of the state's urban population. The council's study became the basis for an initial classification of precincts in Atlanta, and the same procedures were followed the 1960 census tracts of Macon. U.S. Bureau of the Census, *U.S. Census of Population and Housing: 1960, Census Tracts, Macon, Ga., Final Report PHC(1)-86* (Washington, D.C., 1962). Neighborhoods were then further divided along racial lines. The 1950 census tracts of Atlanta were categorized in a similar manner. U.S. Bureau of the Census, *U.S. Census of Population: 1950*, vol. III, *Atlanta, Ga., Census Tract*

low status occupations, but a neighborhood composed of persons in this category was not precisely a "working class district" since the lack of salable skills made unemployment and underemployment serious problems. Generally, members of this class of voters lived in or on the border of outright poverty.

2. White Working Class. Members of this group differed from poor whites more in degree than in substance. Low levels of education and modest incomes were characteristic features. Most males worked in blue collar occupations, often in a semi-skilled capacity. Although unemployment rates were higher than for any other white group except the poor white class, neighborhoods in this category did possess the socio-economic characteristics popularly associated with the term "working class."

3. Middle Income White. Precincts of this type, while relatively heterogeneous, might also have been termed "working class." A majority of employed males labored in blue collar occu-

---

Statistics, Chapter 2 (Washington, D.C., 1952). There were no published census tracts for Macon in 1950, and consequently tracts were ranked on the basis of information reported in the Census of Housing. The factors considered were average value of houses, average monthly rents, conditions of crowding, and extent of dilapidation. U.S. Bureau of the Census, *U.S. Census of Housing: 1950,* vol. V, *Macon, Ga., Block Statistics,* pt. 104 (Washington, D.C., 1952). The relative ranking of neighborhoods in Atlanta and Macon in 1950 was compared to that of 1960, and precinct classifications were adjusted when necessary. Changes and adjustments in precinct classifications in Atlanta during the 1960's were based on: (1) a series of studies sponsored by the Atlanta Community Improvement Program, among the most helpful of which were *Final Report: City of Atlanta, Georgia, Social Report on Neighborhood Analysis* (1967), *Economic Report No. 1: A Demographic Analysis of the City of Atlanta and Its Environs* (1966), *Technical Report: Program for Improvement Action* (1967), *Social Blight and Social Resources Study* (3 vols.; 1967), and *Final Report: City of Atlanta, Georgia, Economic Base/Marketability Summary Report* (1967); (2) Southern Regional Council, *Blueprint for Segregation: A Survey of Atlanta Housing* (Atlanta: Southern Regional Council, 1967); and (3) Atlanta Region Metropolitan Planning Commission, *Population and Housing* (1967). No similar studies existed for Macon, and more informal methods were relied upon. The author is especially indebted to Mr. George Doss of the Macon *Telegraph*, who shared his detailed knowledge of socio-economic conditions within Macon precinct boundaries. The classification of precincts along racial lines in Atlanta was based on voter registration figures, which are maintained by race. In Macon, voting booths were racially segregated prior to the 1964 election, and election returns were reported as "colored" or "white," a procedure that simplified the chores of classification. For the 1964–68 period of Macon politics, the racial composition of prepations, and not infrequently residential areas of this type were relatively new developments. Skilled and semi-skilled blue collar workers were relatively numerous, although this category also included a significant number of white collar employees. A majority of the families earned above $5,000 per year in 1959, and a majority of adults had advanced beyond the eighth grade education level.

4. Semi-Affluent White. This group came closest to typifying the popular stereotype of the middle class. Male employees most frequently worked as skilled wage-earners or in higher level white collar positions. More women served in the labor force than did so in any other white category. Approximately two-thirds of the adults had completed the eighth grade, and an even higher percentage of families enjoyed an income of above $5,000 in 1959.

5. Affluent White. In both Atlanta and Macon, the status residential areas were concentrated in the northern part of the city. The typical family in this category enjoyed an annual income

---

cincts was based on a study of precinct voter registration conducted by Mr. Doss of the Macon *Telegraph*. Most of the precincts used in this study contained a population composed of 90 percent or more of one racial group. The necessity of classifying a sufficient number of precincts to provide an adequate sample of voters in each socio-economic category required in a few instances the relaxation of this standard, but in all cases a precinct containing less than 75 percent of one racial group was discarded. On the basis of sources cited in this note, precinct categories were held constant despite demographic and socio-economic changes within each city and despite changes in or the redrawing of precinct boundaries on four occasions between 1952 and 1968 in Atlanta and on two occasions between 1948 and 1968 in Macon. At the same time, it should also be made clear that census tracts and Community Improvement Program planning areas rarely coincided with precinct boundary lines. Precincts too heterogeneous in socio-economic characteristics to be classified were discarded. In Atlanta, a sufficient number of precincts existed for the author to be relatively selective. In Macon for the years 1948-54, however, only nine precincts (militia districts) served the white voters of the entire county (six additional polling places were available to Negroes). This number was increased to thirteen white precincts and seven (later nine) segregated Negro precincts for the years 1956-62. After 1962 a total of 36 integrated precincts existed. Consequently, precincts in Macon during the 1948-54 period were quite heterogeneous, and classifications are imprecise. For the 1956-62 period, it was possible to obtain more accurate classifications due to fortuitous precinct boundaries and segregated polling places. After 1962, classifications are also substantially accurate. Included among the Macon precincts, however, are all or parts of three militia districts located entirely or partially outside the city limits.

of approximately $10,000, and a majority of adults had received some education beyond high school. A significant proportion of males labored in professional and technical occupations.

6. Poor Black. The socio-economic characteristics for this group were the same as those for the poor white category, although poor blacks were far more numerous than poor whites. In Atlanta in 1960, two-thirds of the families existing on less than $3,000 per year were Negro. Precincts of this type were most often located in or near the central city in both Atlanta and Macon.

7. Nonpoor Black. Although both Atlanta and Macon contain relatively affluent Negro neighborhoods, the most prosperous predominately black precincts were the socio-economic equals of the white middle income areas. These precincts were the most difficult to hold constant. The rapid expansion of the black community during the 1950's and 1960's, especially in Atlanta, led to the deterioration of older Negro middle class neighborhoods and the creation of new ones in formerly white-occupied residential communities. Consequently, any Negro precinct that did not rank in the lowest category was assigned "nonpoor" status, a ranking that combined the characteristics of the white working class and the middle income white categories. The difficulties encountered in holding nonpoor black precincts constant and the discovery that socio-economic characteristics made little apparent difference in the voting tendencies of Negro citizens led to the dropping of this category in the classification of Macon precincts. All black voters in Macon were included in a single category. In Atlanta, the seven category classification was retained for the years 1954–68.

These categories do not contain numerically equal groups of voters. Census tracts were initially divided into quintiles and then were further subdivided along racial lines. Black neighborhoods concentrated in the lower socio-economic categories, whereas a disproportionate share of white precincts qualified for a higher socio-economic ranking. In 1956 approximately 20 percent of the registered voters in Fulton County were Negroes. By 1964 this figure had increased to 27.5 percent, and in the fall of 1969 it was 31.5 percent of the county's total voter registration. In the city of Atlanta, 27 percent of all registered voters were black in 1956, and in 1969 approximately 40 percent were Negroes. The re-districted

Fifth Congressional District, which includes most of Fulton County, contained a registered voting population that was just under 30 percent Negro in 1968. In Bibb County (Macon) black voters cast 14.5 percent of the total county vote in the gubernatorial election of 1950, 14.8 percent in the presidential election of 1956, and 17.3 percent in the 1962 gubernatorial election. Negro registered voters made up 24 percent of the Bibb County total in 1966.

The political inclinations of these various categories of voters are suggested in Table 3-1, which records the results of four selected elections. The referendums on the 1952 constitutional amendment supplementing the county unit system and on the

Table 3-1

Percentage of Conservative Votes in Selected Elections, Atlanta and Macon

Election	Poor White	Working Class White	Middle Income White	Semi- Affluent White	Affluent White	Black Poor	Black Nonpoor
Atlanta							
For County Unit—1952	46.2	29.7	25.1	18.7	17.9		2.5
For Private Schools—1954	61.3	61.8	51.6	38.8	33.8	6.9	7.8
Against Liquor by the Drink—1964	54.4	47.7	58.3	47.5	20.5	19.0	14.8
Against Fluoridation—1968	48.6	43.1	43.7	37.3	22.3	23.2	21.8
Macon*							
For County Unit—1952	55.4	57.0	46.7	37.0	34.6		3.8
For Private Schools—1954	64.5	63.8	57.1	48.2	46.6		12.2

*Includes all or parts of three militia districts located entirely or partially outside t city limits of Macon.

Source: In this and other tables, all precinct returns in Macon are from the Ma *Telegraph* or the Macon *News*. Atlanta precinct returns for the years 1952-65 are f the Atlanta *Constitution*, the Atlanta *Journal*, or the Georgia Department of Arch and History. For the years 1966-68, Atlanta precinct returns are from the office of Fulton County elections supervisor.

1954 "private school plan" amendment authorizing the abandonment of public education in the state posed relatively sharp conservative-progressive conflicts.[3] Two local referendums in Atlanta offered voters an opportunity to express themselves on issues that touched upon religious and intellectual orientation. In 1964 Atlantans endorsed the sale of liquor by the drink despite the lamentable predictions detailed in fundamentalist oratory. Four years later Atlanta voters approved fluoridation of the water supply. Public opposition to this measure came from radical right sources that visualized fluoridation as the handiwork of Communists and atheists and from more moderate opponents who objected to fluoridation on the grounds that it was "forced medication."[4] The votes cast in favor of the county unit amendment and the private school amendment and in opposition to liquor by the drink and fluoridation are listed in Table 3-1.

Urban voters grouped themselves into three relatively stable divisions. The lower status whites were the most conservative of urban voters. They shared many of the attitudes, values, and political inclinations of rural and small town citizens. Members of the three least economically and educationally privileged urban white categories cast above 25 percent of their votes in favor of the county unit system and a majority in support of the possible abandonment of the public school system. They voted above 40 percent in opposition to the sale of liquor by the drink and to the fluoridation of the water supply. The less affluent whites tended to be intolerant in matters pertaining to racial relations and civil liberties, fundamentalist in religion, and generally provincial in outlook.

[3] The 1960 referendum on the "free" electors provision that permitted Democratic presidential electors to place their own judgment above the will of the voters who elected them (which was used as a conservative-progressive voting tendency indicator election in chapter 2) was dropped because precinct election tallies were unobtainable for Atlanta, and in Macon every voter category cast roughly the same majority in favor of the provision. Insofar as this peculiar unanimity on the part of Macon voters represented an endorsement of southern political independence, the vote was, of course, extremely pertinent. This does not seem to have been the case, however. Confusion over the word "free" and local political circumstances apparently accounted for these very atypical election returns.

[4] See the Atlanta *Constitution*, November 4, 1968.

Numerous studies have demonstrated the inverse relationship between socio-economic status and racial toleration.[5] Of all Americans, those white southerners with limited educations, blue collar occupational status, and low incomes were most likely to demonstrate racial prejudice and to hold unfavorable views of Negroes. Less affluent whites tended to visualize themselves as the group most "threatened" by black advancement, and the fear of status deprivation and economic competition strengthened their anti-Negro biases. In the South as well as in the nation, one study reported, "the heart of resistance to change in racial matters . . . rests squarely among the low-income whites."[6] These basic attitudes also carried over into the general field of civil liberties. Lower status southerners were more intolerant than other Americans in their attitudes toward the rights of socialists, Communists, atheists, and other nonconformists.[7] Civil rights, whether defined in terms of minority advancement or individual liberty, found little popular support among poorer whites.

Lower status citizens were relatively less informed about and more isolated from the democratic process. They tended to rely on tradition, take a negative view toward change and innovation, and adopt a defensive and distrustful attitude toward those in power.[8] Professor Alvin Boskoff found from his study of political attitudes of voters in DeKalb County, which includes part of At-

[5] Matthews and Prothro, *New Southern Politics*, pp. 342–66, 396–400, 473–79; Alfred O. Hero, Jr., *The Southerner and World Affairs* (Baton Rouge: Louisiana State University Press, 1965), pp. 383–434; Seymour Martin Lipset, *Political Man: The Social Bases of Politics* (Garden City: Doubleday, 1960), pp. 87–126; William Brink and Louis Harris, *Black and White: A Study of U.S. Racial Attitudes Today* (New York: Simon and Schuster, 1967), pp. 117–39; Melvin M. Tumin and others, *Desegregation: Resistance and Readiness* (Princeton: Princeton University Press, 1958), pp. 80–196; Paul B. Sheatsley, "White Attitudes Toward the Negro," *Daedalus* 95 (Winter, 1966): 217–38; Herbert H. Hyman and Paul B. Sheatsley, "Attitudes Toward Desegregation," *Scientific American* 211 (July, 1964): 2–9.

[6] Brink and Harris, *Black and White*, p. 136.

[7] Samuel A. Stouffer, *Communism, Conformity, and Civil Liberties: A Cross-Section of the Nation Speaks Its Mind* (Garden City: Doubleday, 1955), pp. 109–30.

[8] Lipset, *Political Man*, pp. 103–5; Herbert McClosky, "Conservatism and Personality," *American Political Science Review* 52 (March, 1958): 27–45; Brink and Harris, *Black and White*, pp. 117–39.

lanta, that lower status whites were not only more poorly informed than higher status citizens but were more negative and defensive in their attitudes toward civic affairs. The poorer whites tended to be anti-establishment and to express disparaging views concerning the honesty and character of the politicians.[9]

More so than other citizens, the less socially and economically privileged were apt to belong to fundamentalist religious sects. "Relatively speaking," investigators found in a study of race relations and religious institutions in one southern city, "the sect segregationist is insulated by his social and cultural milieu from the prevailing interpretations of the American creed."[10] During the late 1950's in Atlanta, the fundamentalist ministers of small sect churches in lower status neighborhoods formed the Evangelical Christian Council to propagate their views concerning Jehovah's commandments and the righteousness of racial segregation.[11] Religious fundamentalism, with its pessimistic view of human nature and secular progress, tended to reinforce already prevalent beliefs.

The same less affluent whites who were most conservative on matters pertaining to racial toleration, religion, civil liberties, and acceptance of change also tended to be liberal on economic matters. As Professors Donald R. Matthews and James W. Prothro have observed, "economic conservatism and racial prejudice do *not* tend to go together in the South." On strictly "gut," "bread-and-butter" issues, lower status citizens were more liberal than their affluent neighbors.[12] Increasingly, however, lower status whites in Georgia have forsaken their liberal economic leanings to support traditionalist values. Memories of the Great Depression have faded as the Negro revolution has become, in the opinion of many whites, ever more menacing. Professor Alfred O. Hero has observed an increasing segregationist tendency "to fear that liber-

---

[9] Alvin Boskoff and Harmon Zeigler, *Voting Patterns in a Local Election* (New York: J. B. Lippincott Co., 1964), pp. 89–101.

[10] Ernest Q. Campbell and Thomas F. Pettigrew, *Christians in Racial Crisis: A Study of Little Rock's Ministry* (Washington: Public Affairs Press, 1959), p. 59.

[11] John Wicklein, in the New York *Times*, July 6, 1959.

[12] Matthews and Prothro, *New Southern Politics*, p. 398.

als on economics might also be 'radicals' on race."[13] Certainly Professor Hero's findings are supported by the voting behavior of lower status white citizens residing not only in Georgia's urban neighborhoods but also in the countryside.

The affluent whites were the most progressive of white voters. They cast a substantial majority of their votes in opposition to the county unit system, and they favored the preservation of public education. All categories of Macon voters normally voted more conservatively than the corresponding category of Atlanta voters, but, relatively speaking, progressivism resided in the upper class in both communities. In local referendums, members of the Atlanta affluent class allotted more than three-fourths of their ballots in support of the sale of liquor by the drink and fluoridation. In contrast to other whites, members of the economically and educationally advantaged class had come to terms with the city and, as preceding paragraphs have suggested, were relatively tolerant in their attitudes toward race relations and civil liberties, relatively more likely to have been influenced by modernistic religious doctrine, and, again relatively, more inclined to accept change and to have a progressive view of community affairs.

The progressivism of affluent urbanites should not, of course, be exaggerated. They were less tolerant and more ideologically conservative than their nonsouthern socio-economic peers.[14] On economic issues they were more conservative than lower status whites. Nevertheless, the more affluent urban whites were generally oriented toward civic "progress." As a University of Michigan research team concluded from a national study of political attitudes, "it is the high income people who are relatively *more* willing to pay taxes than have the government postpone doing things that need to be done."[15] Unlike lower class whites, the urban affluent class normally supported bond issues for commu-

[13] Hero, *The Southerner and World Affairs*, p. 374.

[14] Lloyd A. Free and Hadley Cantril, *The Political Beliefs of Americans: A Study of Public Opinion* (Brunswick, N.J.: Rutgers University Press, 1967), pp. 1–58; Stouffer, *Communism, Conformity, and Civil Liberties*, pp. 109–30. See also the sources cited in footnote 5 above.

[15] Angus Campbell et al., *The American Voter* (New York: John Wiley and Sons, 1960), p. 196.

nity improvements and was the only group of Atlanta voters to favor the construction of a metropolitan rapid transit system in the 1968 referendum. Professor Boskoff found affluent suburbanites in DeKalb County more informed about governmental affairs and more likely to express positive attitudes concerning community progress than were less affluent citizens.[16] Reconciled to urban life, higher status whites wished to preserve their own positions and to promote a good business and civic atmosphere in Atlanta and Macon. The semi-affluent whites served as something of a buffer zone between poorer white conservatism and wealthier white progressivism.

Negroes were the Georgia liberals. They massively opposed the county unit system and supported desegregated public education. By substantial majorities they endorsed the sale of liquor by the drink and fluoridation. Politically, Negroes were the most urban of all voters and the most self-conscious and united. On both economic and ideological issues, they were far more likely than white citizens to express liberal views.[17] At the same time, however, black liberalism was rooted in a favorable attitude toward racial equality and welfare programs. Educationally disadvantaged and the products of narrow cultural horizons, Negroes possessed many of the same authoritarian tendencies associated with the attitudes of the poorer whites. As Professor Hero has observed, "the Southern Negro, even more than the white, has been unlettered, poor, close to the soil, insulated from events and ideas beyond his community, and convinced that only God could change his fate."[18] Black southerners, in comparison with white southerners, have been found to be more intolerant of the rights of radicals and nonconformists, to exhibit greater tendencies toward authoritarianism, to be less politically informed, and to be

[16] Boskoff and Zeigler, *Voting Patterns in a Local Election*, pp. 57–81; Alvin Boskoff, "Social and Cultural Patterns in a Suburban Area: Their Significance for Urban Change in the South," *Journal of Social Issues* 22 (January, 1966): 85–100.

[17] Jack L. Walker, "Protest and Negotiation: A Case Study of Negro Leadership in Atlanta, Georgia," *Midwest Journal of Political Science* 7 (May, 1963): 99–124; Free and Cantril, *The Political Beliefs of Americans*, pp. 35–36; Hero, *The Southerner and World Affairs*, pp. 504–43; Brink and Harris, *Black and White*, pp. 74–96.

[18] Hero, *The Southerner and World Affairs*, p. 504.

more resistant to the abstract notion of change.[19] Nevertheless, within the context of Georgia political warfare, the quest for social, economic, and status security by black citizens led those voters toward the liberal position on virtually every political issue.

Normally, Negroes and affluent whites cooperated politically. Georgia's richest people—the affluent urban-suburban whites—and the state's poorest people, the Negroes, banded together against the middling whites in a somewhat unnatural but nevertheless effective alliance. This coalition has dominated local politics in Atlanta since World War II.[20] Table 3-2 records the conservative

Table 3-2

Percentage of Conservative Votes in Atlanta Mayoralty Elections

Election	Poor White	Working Class White	Middle Income White	Semi-Affluent White	Affluent White	Poor Black	Non-poor Black
Maddox—1957	67.3	68.8	64.7	57.4	28.6	3.1	2.4
Maddox—First Primary, 1961	47.7	42.4	40.5	31.1	12.3	1.3	0.8
Maddox—Runoff, 1961	74.6	62.0	71.8	62.3	26.4	1.3	0.4
Smith—1965	59.9	57.4	52.7	51.4	33.0	3.1	3.0

vote by socio-economic category in the nonpartisan mayoralty races of 1957, 1961, and 1965. The coalition favorite in 1957 was William B. Hartsfield. In 1961 and 1965, it was Ivan Allen, Jr. Both Hartsfield and Allen earned national reputations as progressive mayors. The principal anticoalition candidate in the 1957 general election and 1961 primary contest was Lester G. Maddox, an avid proponent of white supremacy in social relations and

[19]Matthews and Prothro, *New Southern Politics*, pp. 265-312; Hero, *The Southerner and World Affairs*, pp. 504-43.

[20]M. Kent Jennings, *Community Influentials: The Elites of Atlanta* (New York: Free Press of Glencoe, 1964); M. Kent Jennings and Harmon Zeigler, "Class, Party, and Race in Four Types of Elections: The Case of Atlanta," *Journal of Politics* 28 (May, 1966): 391-407; Clarence A. Bacote, "The Negro in Atlanta Politics," *Phylon* 16 (Fourth Quarter, 1955): 333-50; Walker, "Negro Voting in Atlanta," 379-87.

fundamentalism in religion.[21] Allen's chief opponent in 1965 was Milton M. Smith, a moderate but the heir to anticoalition support. Hartsfield in 1957 and Allen in 1965 won first primary victories. In 1961, however, none of the five candidates received a first primary majority, and Allen and Maddox went into a bitterly fought runoff campaign from which Allen ultimately emerged victorious.

Generally, political warfare in Georgia has involved white candidates. Whether the coalition would remain intact in support of black contenders for top-level offices is an open question. The coalition has sometimes held together behind Negro candidates in the past. In 1953 it placed on the board of education Dr. Rufus E. Clement, a Negro and president of Atlanta University. The lower status whites, however, have consistently opposed Negro aspirants. Q. V. Williamson, a highly regarded Negro businessman, sought a position on the Atlanta board of aldermen in 1961 and again in 1965. In both years his chief opponent was Jimmy Vickers, who by 1965 had been convicted of bribery and whose performance as an alderman had been publicly criticized by Mayor Allen.[22] Williamson lost in 1961, but in his runoff contest with Vickers in 1965, coalition support materialized and Williamson emerged victorious. The 1965 runoff contest thus provided a choice between an attractive Negro candidate who espoused progressive views and a publicly discredited white contender who projected a conservative image. In both 1961 and 1965 Vickers won more than two-thirds of the total votes of the less affluent whites.

In state politics the urban areas persistently showed the greatest sympathy for progressive causes, and this progressivism resulted from the votes of Negroes and affluent whites. Lower status whites exhibited political inclinations only slightly less conservative than those of the whites of the countryside. The Talmadge faction within the state Democratic party thus found a significant minority of loyal city followers. In 1948 Herman Talmadge ran extremely well in the white neighborhoods of Macon, and in 1950

[21] See Bruce Galphin, *The Riddle of Lester Maddox* (Atlanta: Camelot, 1968).

[22] Eugene Patterson, in the Atlanta *Constitution*, August 25, 1965; Atlanta *Journal*, September 9–17, 1965.

Table 3-3

Percentage of Conservative Votes in Atlanta Aldermanic Elections

Election	Poor White	Working Class White	Middle Income White	Semi-Affluent White	Affluent White	Poor Black	Non-poor Black
Vickers, 1961	72.7	74.6	83.9	80.3	58.6	5.9	3.6
Vickers, Runoff, 1965	76.7	66.1	67.9	66.4	40.3	2.1	2.3

he won a majority of the votes of the two lowest socio-economic categories of whites and over 40 percent of the middle income and semi-affluent whites. In 1954 voters in the three least affluent white categories marked a majority of their ballots for Marvin Griffin or Tom Linder. The votes of Negroes and higher status whites kept Bibb County in the anti-Talmadge camp in 1948 and 1950. Griffin captured Bibb County's unit votes in 1954 by winning a plurality in an election that included nine candidates.

Table 3-4

Percentage of Votes Received by Talmadge Candidates in Macon

Election	Poor White	Working Class White	Middle Income White	Semi-Affluent White	Affluent White	Black
Talmadge, 1948	70.6	77.9	61.5	52.2	46.6	0.4
Talmadge, 1950	54.4	59.3	47.0	42.4	34.6	1.3
Griffin–Linder, 1954	62.1	63.1	56.4	44.7	41.6	2.6

When Marvin Griffin sought another term as governor in 1962, the ensuing campaign offered a relatively clear choice between conservatism and progressivism. Griffin remained what he had always been, a county unit politician filled with homely sayings, a spoils politician whose administration had come under attack for corruption, a segregationist politician who continued to defend the values of south Georgia whites.[23] His opponent was Carl Sanders of Augusta who projected a progressive image. Although Sanders assured voters that "I am a segregationist," he

[23] See Bartley, *The Rise of Massive Resistance*, pp. 68–72.

stated that he believed in equal opportunity and generally took a "moderate" position on the race issue.[24] In the context of the times, Sanders' endorsement of equal opportunity and his generally progressive platform qualified him for a position far to the left of Griffin. Most of the state's political leaders and newspapers supported Sanders, as did Negroes and the more affluent urban whites. Griffin still aroused considerable enthusiasm among lower status whites. In Macon he won majorities in four of the five white categories of voters, and only the overwhelming opposition of Negroes and the more wealthy whites saved the county for Sanders. In Atlanta, Griffin fared badly, but he received more than 35 percent of the votes in the three least affluent white categories.

The Talmadge faction candidates in 1948, 1950, and 1954, and Griffin in 1962, appealed to the same categories of voters that had demonstrated the greatest support for the county unit amendment and had shown the least concern for public education. The continuity of these voting alignments in Macon is suggested in Table 3-5.

Table 3-5

Correlations between the Vote for Conservative Gubernatorial Candidates and the Conservative Vote in Selected Elections in Macon

	Pro County Unit Amendment	Pro Private School Amendment
Herman Talmadge, 1948	.9955	.9940
Herman Talmadge, 1950	.9924	.9911
Griffin–Linder, 1954	.9948	.9989
Griffin, 1962	.9147	.9296

Correlations are product moment correlations based on six (or, in the case of Atlanta, seven) categories of voters: poor white, working class white, middle income white, semi-affluent white, affluent white, and black (or poor black and nonpoor black for Atlanta voting correlations).

In presidential politics, the most conservative voters showed the greatest enthusiasm for the party of liberalism, and the most progressive white citizens preferred the conservative party. The Democratic party consistently appealed most strongly to the lower

[24] As quoted in the Atlanta *Constitution*, August 16, 1962.

socio-economic class of whites. The Great Depression had rein-
forced the poorer whites' identification with the Democratic party
in the South as elsewhere in the nation. The more affluent whites,
influenced by the growing prosperity of the 1940's and 1950's,
had drifted far from their Democratic moorings. During the
1950's, upper income whites in Atlanta consistently gave a majority of their votes to the G.O.P. The affluent class of whites in
Macon was somewhat more reluctant to abandon the Democrats,
and not until 1960 did the Republican ticket win a majority
among upper income voters. Negroes were the least stable of all
Georgia voters vis-à-vis the national parties. In 1948 and 1952 they
voted Democratic. In 1956 they massively defected to the Republican column. In Atlanta, black voters remained with the
G.O.P. in 1960; in Macon they rejoined the Democrats.

Table 3-6

Percentage of Votes Received by Democratic Presidential Candidates in Atlanta and
Macon

Election	Poor White	Working Class White	Middle Income White	Semi-Affluent White	Affluent White	Black Poor	Black Nonpoor
Atlanta							
Stevenson, 1952	80.1	72.2	65.7	65.2	35.7	74.3	
Stevenson, 1956	77.9	67.1	77.9	75.1	49.2	15.6	12.2
Kennedy, 1960	64.8	62.2	58.9	59.9	42.3	43.0	40.3
Macon							
Stevenson, 1952	84.8	75.6	77.7	53.5	61.3	85.6	
Stevenson, 1956	85.6	76.3	82.3	68.7	57.3	36.3	
Kennedy, 1960	68.0	61.6	65.1	60.3	46.8	63.4	

The growth of a Republican party in Georgia threatened the
alliance between poor blacks and wealthy whites. In state and
local elections, this coalition had lent a progressive cast to urban
politics that the adamant opposition of lower status whites usually
failed to overcome. But the affluent whites found it much easier
to identify with the Republican party than did Negroes. Black
voters showed considerable enthusiasm for the G.O.P. during the
mid-1950's. In 1956 General Eisenhower won more than 60 percent of the Negro vote in Macon and more than 80 percent in

Atlanta. In that same year, black citizens in Atlanta favored a Republican congressional candidate with approximately 90 percent of their votes. Republican Randolph W. Thrower challenged incumbent Representative James C. Davis in the bloated Fifth Congressional District, which included Fulton, DeKalb, and Rockdale Counties. Davis possessed a reactionary voting record in the House of Representatives and was a fiery proponent of the virtues of white supremacy.[25] Although his most loyal adherents resided in DeKalb and Rockdale Counties, he commanded the allegiance of a substantial lower class white following in Fulton County. Thrower swept the black precincts and won a majority in upper income districts; however, Davis received more than two-thirds of the votes cast by citizens in the other four white categories and carried both Fulton County and the election.

Six years later Charles L. Weltner, a young, articulate Atlanta lawyer, opposed Davis in the Democratic primary. Weltner espoused a generally progressive program that contrasted sharply with Davis' congressional record and campaign oratory. Weltner won a slight plurality of the votes, but two minor candidates forced a runoff contest. Weltner won the second primary by a clear majority and then faced a Republican contender in the general election. James O'Callaghan, the G.O.P. nominee, was staunchly conservative in his views toward government and the economy, but he did not take an overtly racist position.[26] The results in the two primary elections and the general election are shown in Table 3-7.

In both primary elections every category of white voters except the most affluent presumably viewed with favor Davis and his record as a defender of the economic interests of the wealthy and the social interests of whites. The affluent whites gave Weltner a slight majority, and Negroes massively rallied to the Weltner cause. In the general election, however, the lower status whites joined

[25] For example, see Georgia Commission on Education, *Congressman James C. Davis Speaks to the States' Rights Council* (Atlanta: Georgia Commission on Education, 1956).

[26] M. Kent Jennings and L. Harmon Zeigler, "A Moderate's Victory in a Southern Congressional District," *Public Opinion Quarterly* 28 (Winter, 1964): 595–603; Charles Longstreet Weltner, *Southerner* (New York: J. B. Lippincott Co., 1966), pp. 45–53.

Table 3-7

Percentage of Votes Received by Major Candidates in Fifth District Congressional Races
 in Atlanta, 1962

Candidate	Poor White	Working Class White	Middle Income White	Semi-Affluent White	Affluent White	Poor Black	Non-poor Black
First Primary							
Weltner	37.4	37.1	36.4	42.6	51.2	78.5	82.3
Davis	54.7	54.6	54.2	52.1	45.3	11.0	7.7
Other	7.9	8.4	9.4	5.3	3.5	10.5	9.9
Runoff Primary							
Weltner	39.8	46.0	41.8	45.2	51.5	96.4	98.1
Davis	60.2	54.0	58.2	54.8	48.5	3.6	1.9
General Election							
Weltner	67.4	66.3	64.0	61.6	40.5	70.3	68.3
O'Callaghan	32.6	33.7	36.0	38.4	59.5	29.7	31.7

Weltner, and the upper status whites abandoned him. The reason
for the shift was, of course, party identification. The lower status
whites preferred Davis to Weltner, but they also preferred a Democrat to a member of the party of Thaddeus Stevens and Herbert
Hoover. The affluent whites, on the other hand, favored a progressive Democrat over a conservative one, but they also favored a
conservative Republican over a progressive Democrat. Negroes remained loyal to the progressive candidate in all three elections.

The coalition of affluent whites and Negroes had made the
city safe for progressivism. Nonpartisan local elections and primary contests on the local and state level that clearly pitted a
progressive candidate against a conservative candidate normally
brought predictable voting alignments.[27] The stability of the progressive coalition in Atlanta is reviewed in Table 3-8, which records the correlations between the votes cast in selected elections
involving a conservative-progressive division. As the correlations
show, Atlanta voting patterns remained notably consistent.

The rise of a two-party system, however, brought to a head
the conflicts of interest between poor blacks and affluent whites,

[27]There were, of course, exceptions. For example, the affluent whites
failed to support Morris Abram when he opposed James Davis in the 1954
Fifth District race (presumably because of Abram's Jewish religion). On the
other hand, Bodenhamer's avid racism failed to spark much of a response
among the poorer whites in the 1958 gubernatorial campaign.

Table 3-8

Correlations between the Progressive Votes in Selected Elections in Atlanta

	Referendums			Democratic Primaries	
Referendums	Against Private School Amendment 1954	For Liquor by the Drink 1964	For Fluoridation 1968	Sanders 1962 Gubernatorial	Weltner 1962 Congres. Runoff
Against Private School Amendment, 1954	——	.8796	.9036	.9709	.9266
For Liquor by the Drink, 1964	.8796	——	.9700	.9480	.8356
For Fluoridation, 1968	.9036	.9700	——	.9423	.7843
Democratic Primaries					
Sanders, Gubernatorial, 1962	.9709	.9480	.9423	——	.9450
Weltner, Congressional Runoff, 1962	.9266	.8356	.7843	.9450	——
City Elections					
Hartsfield, Mayoralty, 1957	.9686	.9521	.9366	.9870	.9358
Allen, Mayoralty Runoff, 1961	.9408	.9738	.9459	.9913	.9321
Allen, Mayoralty, 1965	.9740	.9192	.9048	.9877	.9638
Williamson, Aldermanic Runoff, 1965	.9551	.8770	.8961	.9895	.9738
Partisan Elections					
Thrower, Congressional, 1956	.9300	.9425	.8919	.9800	.9670
Eisenhower, Presidential, 1956	.9227	.9283	.8739	.9758	.9751
Nixon, Presidential, 1960	.8945	.9599	.9785	.9399	.8070
O'Callaghan, Congressional, 1962	-.0715	.2136	.3117	-.0212	-.3339

between inner city ghettos and outer city ranch-style houses and apartments. Affluent whites, as Samuel Lubell has observed, "identified the South's economic future with the interests of business" and tended to view the G.O.P. as the party of a good business atmosphere.[28] "The young lawyer searching for clients," Lubell wrote, "the college graduate seeking a supervisory post in the mills, merchants and salesmen with something to sell, bankers hunting new investment outlets for growing deposits, doctors

[28] Samuel Lubell, *White and Black: The Test of a Nation* (New York: Harper and Row, 1964), p. 69.

Table 3-8 (continued)

	City Elections			Partisan Elections			
Hartsfield Mayoralty 1957	Allen Mayoralty Runoff 1961	Allen Mayoralty 1965	Williamson Aldermanic Runoff 1965	Thrower 1956 Congressional	Eisenhower 1956 Presidential	Nixon 1960 Presidential	O'Callaghan 1962 Congressional
.9686	.9408	.9740	.9551	.9300	.9227	.8945	-.0715
.9521	.9738	.9192	.9237	.9425	.9283	.9599	.2136
.9366	.9459	.9048	.8961	.8919	.8739	.9785	.3117
.9870	.9913	.9877	.9895	.9800	.9758	.9399	-.0212
.9358	.9321	.9638	.9738	.9670	.9751	.8070	-.3339
——	.9886	.9932	.9847	.9813	.9717	.9512	.0041
.9886	——	.9804	.9862	.9897	.9834	.9516	.0231
.9932	.9803	——	.9946	.9839	.9795	.9273	-.0906
.9847	.9862	.9946	——	.9936	.9930	.9170	-.1177
.9813	.9897	.9839	.9936	——	.9986	.9133	-.1020
.9717	.9834	.9795	.9930	.9986	——	.8962	-.1432
.9512	.9516	.9273	.9170	.9133	.8962	——	.2755
.0041	.0231	-.0906	-.1177	-.1020	-.1432	.2755	——

building their practice, all the numerous property holders who hope the cities they live in will grow out to the land they own and strike them rich—all are building their dream castles upon the growth of industry."[29] The "dream castles" of Negroes, needless to add, were often built of different stuff. As the national Democratic party became ever more identified as the champion of civil rights, Negro voters increasingly shifted back into the Democratic camp. Black Republicanism reached its peak in 1956, and, there-

[29] Samuel Lubell, *The Future of American Politics* (2d rev. ed.; Garden City: Doubleday, 1956), pp. 118-19.

after, there was a growing separation between the voting inclinations of Negroes and of affluent whites.

So long as the lower status whites remained true to the Democratic party, Negroes found themselves in an advantageous political position. They could, as they did in the 1962 Fifth District race, join with the affluent whites to nominate a progressive Democrat and then could join with the poorer whites to elect him. But for the same reasons that Negroes found the national Democrats increasingly attractive, the lower status whites demonstrated a diminishing affection for the Democratic party. The growing good will displayed toward the Republican party by virtually all categories of whites is indicated in Table 3-6 above; this tendency was invigorated by the Goldwater campaign of 1964.

Republicanism
and Mr. Goldwater

In the broadest sense, five overlapping but still identifiable voting "blocs" lay at the base of Georgia politics. The rural Georgia countryside and the towns of south and central Georgia contained a predominately conservative voting population. These citizens shared common assumptions with the less economically and educationally privileged whites of the city. Segregationist in social matters, fundamentalist in religion, and traditionalist in outlook, these two broad groupings of voters tended to join together in opposition to the urban-progressive-modernistic notions of Negroes and affluent whites. In the city the poorer, more traditionalist whites were a minority; in the countryside they were the majority.[1] Consequently, Georgia politics demonstrated a frequent rural-urban cleavage.

[1] While attitudinal differences between upper and lower status whites in the countryside were no doubt less marked than they were in the city, avail-

The affluent whites in the cities, suburbs, and larger towns represented another and a growing voting force. In the most general sense, members of this class held common assumptions about economic progress and the maintenance of a good business atmosphere and a respectable national image. Of all whites they tended to be the most modernistic in their religious views and the most tolerant on the racial question. Negroes also rejected rural Georgia traditionalism, especially urban Negroes who, unlike their country relatives, voted on a substantial scale prior to the 1960's and during the 1960's voted with less fear of intimidation and less concern for the reaction of their white neighbors. The coalition of poor Negroes and rich whites accounted, to a considerable degree, for the more progressive stance that set the city apart politically from the countryside. The "welfare economics" policies preferred by Negroes were, however, vastly different from the "good government" programs in support of a good business atmosphere and efficiency in government that appealed to the affluent whites. Nor did affluent white toleration on racial matters necessarily lead to the same policies as black insistence on racial equalitarianism. Consequently, the alliance between affluent whites and Negroes was intrinsically less stable than the opposition coalition of the poorer whites of city and countryside.

The fifth voting group resided in north Georgia. Enjoying substantially greater prosperity and economic growth than other small town inhabitants in the state gave Piedmont townsmen a greater stake in the real world of the present and tended to counter devotion to tradition. The predominately white residents of the hill country were less immediately concerned with racial issues, and the north Georgia towns only occasionally demonstrated the same dedication to the social and ideological status quo that dominated the voting tendencies of the south Georgia towns. The same Unionist-Scalawag-Populist tradition that had left its mark upon upland whites in other southern states may have also

---

able evidence clearly indicates that the poorer farmers offered significantly greater support to candidates of the Talmadge faction and other conservative alternatives in state politics than did relatively more prosperous merchants and proprietors in the towns. Bernd, *Grass Roots Politics*, p. 23; Pyles, "Race and Ruralism in Georgia Elections," 70–77, 100. See Table 4-1 in this chapter.

influenced north Georgia voters. In any case, rural north Georgia was less conservative than the rural areas to the south, and north Georgia townsmen were likely to join affluent urbanites in support of a politics of progressivism.

These group voting patterns, while very general and subject to numerous local exceptions, had remained remarkably consistent. Table 4-1 reviews a number of the elections discussed in chapters 2 and 3.[2] The Talmadge faction and, after its demise as a functioning entity, individual conservative candidates appealed most strongly to citizens of south and central Georgia, to the lower socio-economic levels of white voters in the cities, and to rural voters in north Georgia. These same voters, joined by the north Georgia townsmen, provided the national Democratic party with its overwhelming majorities in presidential elections. The loyalty displayed by the state's most conservative voters toward the nation's most liberal party was, as Jasper Shannon wrote in a somewhat different context, "a species of ancestor worship without meaning in contemporary political action."[3] As the Great Depression faded into history and as the Democratic party under John F. Kennedy solidified its position as the champion of minority rights, the paradox became increasingly untenable.

This situation assured the success of Barry M. Goldwater's "southern strategy" in Georgia. Professor Bernard Cosman, in his study of the Goldwater campaign in the South, noted that "in 1964 the Republican presidential party, for the first time in history, played the role of the 'traditional' party of the South. . . ." Goldwater, who voted against the 1964 civil rights bill, campaigned on a state's rights platform. Many white voters in the Deep South, Cosman observed, "responded much as their grandfathers would have. They voted for what they perceived to be the 'candidate of the southern white man.' "[4]

[2] Also included in Table 4-1 is the 1966 Democratic primary runoff election for lieutenant governor. That election was a hard-fought contest between Peter Zack Geer, the avidly conservative incumbent, and George T. Smith, who combined a relatively progressive platform with an effective "common man" political style.

[3] Shannon, *Toward a New Politics in the South*, p. 15.

[4] Bernard Cosman, *Five States for Goldwater: Continuity and Change in Southern Voting Patterns* (University, Ala.: University of Alabama Press, 1966), pp. 55, 62.

Table 4-1

Table 4-1. Percentage of Votes Received by Selected Candidates in Georgia, Atlanta, and Macon, 1948-66

Democratic Primaries	South (rural) (town)	Black Belt (rural) (town)	North (rural) (town)	14 Urban Cos.	Fulton County (Atl.)		Poor White	Working Class White	Middle Income White	Semi-Affluent White	Affluent White	Poor	Black Poor	Black Nonpoor
Talmadge, 1948, Gov.	60.8 (62.8) (58.0)	58.6 (59.3) (55.1)	52.2 (55.7) (47.3)	46.2	34.0	Macon:	70.6	77.9	61.5	52.2	46.6			0.4
									(Atlanta returns unobtainable)					
Talmadge, 1950, Gov.	56.6 (59.9) (52.6)	55.0 (56.5) (47.8)	49.7 (53.3) (45.0)	46.2	32.6	Macon:	54.4	59.3	47.0	42.4	34.6			1.3
									(Atlanta returns unobtainable)					
Linder-Griffin, 1954, Gov.	60.5 (62.8) (57.3)	55.9 (56.2) (54.5)	55.8 (59.1) (51.7)	39.9	31.3	Macon:	62.1	63.1	56.4	44.7	41.6			2.6
									(Atlanta returns unobtainable)					
Griffin, 1962, Gov.	51.0 (54.9) (46.1)	54.4 (54.2) (55.8)	40.7 (44.5) (36.0)	31.7	22.1	Atlanta:	45.2	36.6	38.6	32.0	18.2	0.8		0.5
						Macon:	51.2	53.5	54.0	54.1	31.4			1.0
Geer, 1966, Lt. Gov.	55.6 (61.5) (48.9)	51.4 (52.4) (46.8)	48.6 (52.1) (44.4)	40.8	27.0	Atlanta:	47.5	45.9	42.1	37.9	22.1	8.3	21.4	6.0
						Macon:	52.0	55.3	50.8	54.3	39.5			
Amendment Elections														
For County Unit, 1952	67.5 (74.8) (58.5)	61.4 (64.1) (49.6)	47.9 (54.1) (40.5)	35.8	29.4	Atlanta:	46.2	29.7	25.1	18.7	17.9	6.9		2.5
						Macon:	55.4	57.0	46.7	37.0	34.6			3.8
For Private Schools, 1954	68.2 (73.4) (61.5)	64.7 (66.4) (57.8)	54.1 (55.8) (52.0)	44.2	41.8	Atlanta:	61.3	61.8	51.6	38.8	33.8		12.2	7.8
						Macon:	64.5	63.8	57.1	48.2	46.6			12.2
Presidential Elections														
Stevenson, 1952	77.6 (79.5) (75.2)	77.2 (78.9) (69.1)	75.4 (73.6) (77.4)	60.2	59.8	Atlanta:	80.1	72.2	65.7	65.2	35.7	15.6	74.3	2.5
						Macon:	84.8	75.6	77.7	53.5	61.3		85.6	3.8
Stevenson, 1956	79.6 (81.7) (77.1)	77.1 (78.4) (71.6)	68.5 (67.1) (70.3)	57.5	56.0	Atlanta:	77.9	67.1	77.9	75.1	49.2	15.6	36.3	12.2
						Macon:	85.6	76.3	82.3	68.7	57.3			12.2
Kennedy, 1960	72.7 (74.2) (71.0)	73.5 (74.8) (67.7)	68.8 (68.8) (68.7)	53.2	50.8	Atlanta:	64.8	62.2	58.9	59.9	42.3	43.0	63.4	40.3
						Macon:	68.0	61.6	65.1	60.3	46.8			

Georgia Republicans mounted an extensive state-wide campaign in support of Goldwater's candidacy, and they qualified five congressional candidates and numerous contenders for local offices. The pary fueled these efforts with substantial financial and organizational resources. The G.O.P. also benefited from divisions within the Democratic camp. Governor Carl B. Sanders worked energetically for Lyndon B. Johnson's election, but few other state-level Democrats showed much enthusiasm for the national party ticket. Senators Herman Talmadge and Richard Russell gave only token support to the Democratic cause, while other conservative Democratic spokesmen, such as Marvin Griffin and Roy V. Harris of Augusta, endorsed Goldwater. In the south and central portions of the state, organized efforts on Johnson's behalf failed to materialize in the face of Goldwater's popularity and the overt hostility felt by many local leaders toward the civil rights and Great Society programs of the Johnson administration.[5]

The Goldwater candidacy disrupted normal partisan voting patterns in the state. In the countryside Goldwater ran best in the south and central Georgia lowlands, past citadels of Democratic strength. More than 60 percent of the voters in the black belt and the south marked their ballots for the Republican candidate. Goldwater fared less well in the hills and mountains to the north. There the racial issues that dominated voter response in the lowlands were less immediate, and such federally sponsored programs as the Tennessee Valley Authority enjoyed greater popularity. Not surprisingly, there was a high correlation (.9516) between the Goldwater vote in 1964 and the vote for the Dixiecrat ticket in 1948. Both appealed most strongly to citizens residing in the lowlands.

The Georgia G.O.P. concentrated its quest for congressional seats in the northern part of the state. Apparently misinterpreting the nature of Goldwater's appeal, the Republicans offered serious competition in all four of the congressional districts in the Atlanta area and to the north. They competed for only one of the six congressional seats in the south and central portions of the state, and only in that contest was their campaign successful. Howard H. "Bo" Callaway, the heir to a textile fortune, carried Muscogee County (Columbus) and won 11 of the 16 rural and small town

[5] Atlanta *Journal*, October 1–November 8, 1964.

counties in the Third Congressional District. Had the Republicans chosen to focus their congressional ambitions in the south, where Goldwater was strongest, rather than in the Atlanta area and to the north, where Goldwater was weakest, they might well have been rewarded with a greater measure of success. Nevertheless, Goldwater and Callaway demonstrated that the Democratic party's heretofore unshakable position in south and central Georgia was, after all, not immune to Republican attack.

In the cities, Goldwater broke the Negro–affluent-white coalition. Black voters massively endorsed Lyndon B. Johnson, while a substantial majority of affluent whites joined the Goldwater crusade. At the same time, lower status whites shifted to presidential Republicanism. In the backlash following the sit-in movement, civil rights demonstrations, and passage of the 1964 civil rights law, the poorer whites joined south and central Georgia citizens in rejecting the Democratic ticket. Urban voting patterns thus pitted black against white voters. Virtually solid Negro opposition denied Goldwater a majority in Atlanta, but he won 58.6 percent of the votes of the other 14 urban counties. In Macon every category of white voters gave Goldwater above two-thirds of its votes.

This same black-versus-white alignment was evident in the Fifth Congressional District election in Atlanta. James O'Callaghan, again challenging Charles Weltner, carried the white vote on every socio-economic level. Against the same opponent in 1962, O'Callaghan had won a majority only among affluent white voters, receiving fewer than 40 percent of the ballots cast by members of any of the other four white categories. At the same time, O'Callaghan had won slightly above 30 percent of the black vote. By 1964 Lyndon Johnson's effective promotion of civil rights legislation and Weltner's vote for the 1964 civil rights bill had combined with the negative images projected by both Goldwater and O'Callaghan to permit the Republican congressional candidate to sweep the white precincts and to lose almost all support in black neighborhoods. Weltner carried approximately 99 percent of the Negro vote in his successful campaign for re-election to the House. Tables 4–2 and 4–3 record the percentage of votes received by Goldwater and O'Callaghan in each voter category.

Table 4-2

Percentage of Votes Received by Republican Presidential Candidate in 1964 in Georgia

Candidate	South (rural) (town)	Black Belt (rural) (town)	North (rural) (town)	14 Urban Cos.	Fulton County (Atl.)
Goldwater, 1964	62.4 (63.3) (61.3)	60.7 (59.4) (66.4)	44.2 (45.0) (43.3)	58.6	43.9

Table 4-3

Percentage of Votes Received by Republican Candidates in 1964 in Atlanta and Macon

Candidate	Poor White	White Working Class	Middle Income White	Semi-Affluent White	Affluent White	Black Poor	Nonpoor
Goldwater							
Atlanta	57.6	56.5	62.5	62.4	57.4	1.2	0.6
Macon	68.3	74.8	68.8	73.5	67.7	13.6*	
O'Callaghan							
Atlanta	55.4	56.9	61.8	62.3	58.2	1.5	1.2

*Prior to 1964 polling places in Macon were segregated by race. The integration of the voting booths in 1964 left the city with no all-black precincts. The 13.6 percent of the black vote received by Goldwater very likely reflects the preference of the white minority residing in predominately Negro districts.

The Goldwater candidacy forged new voting alignments in Georgia, but it also climaxed a trend in Republican voting patterns that had been developing since the mid-1950's. The United States Supreme Court decision ruling against the constitutionality of public school segregation in 1954 had enlivened white concern for the protection of white supremacy. The national Democratic party's outspoken support of civil rights encouraged growing numbers of Negro voters to return to the Democratic fold, but it also led substantial numbers of whites to abandon the party. The sharply contrasting positions taken by Johnson and Goldwater on minority rights brought these trends to culmination. Table 4-4 shows the correlations between the vote for Goldwater and the votes for other Republican candidates.

Leadership changes in the Georgia Republican party kept pace with the G.O.P.'s shifting base of popular support. During the Eisenhower years the Atlanta-oriented Republican leadership had espoused a program that rested broadly on economic conservatism and racial moderation. The party drew support from the same groups that had endorsed the anti-Talmadge faction in state politics. The growth of the Republican party in Georgia, however, served to enhance the position of more conservative spokesmen. Those Georgians repelled by the liberal economic and social justice policies sponsored by the national Democrats gained increasing influence in state party affairs. The emerging leadership was in the Bourbon Democratic tradition. Upper class, oriented toward the non-Atlanta urban areas, ultra-conservative on virtually any economic, social, or ideological issue, the new Republicans won control of the party at the state convention in 1964. In the wake of Goldwater's disastrous national showing at the polls, Georgia Republicans successfully patched up the split between the older, more moderate conservatives and the newer ultra-conservatives.[6] Nevertheless, Goldwater proponents remained in the ascendency, and the Arizonan's quest for the presidency, by providing the rallying point for the new leadership, left the Georgia Republican party more conservative than before.

Table 4-4

Correlations between the Vote for Goldwater and the Votes for Previous Republican Candidates

| | Goldwater | | |
	Georgia	Atlanta	Macon
Eisenhower, 1956	-.5320	-.9506	-.8700
Thrower, 1956 (Fifth Congressional)	——	-.9395	——
Nixon, 1960	-.3638	-.7371	.1453
O'Callaghan, 1962	——	.4324	——
O'Callaghan, 1964	——	.9994	——

[6] Bernard Cosman, *The Case of the Goldwater Delegates: Deep South Republican Leadership* (University, Ala.: University of Alabama Press, 1966), pp. 21-58; Topping, Lazarek, and Linder, *Southern Republicanism*, pp. 60-67.

Goldwater appealed to a coalition of affluent and non-affluent whites in the cities and the inhabitants of the south and central Georgia countryside. The affluent whites identified with the Republican party, and the white residents of the less prestigious neighborhoods of the city and of the towns and rural areas in the Georgia lowlands identified with Goldwater's position on minority rights. Together, they accounted for the greater portion of the ballots that gave the Republican ticket slightly over 54 percent of the state's popular vote. Georgia Republicans made preparations to duplicate Goldwater's winning strategy in the 1966 state and congressional elections, but in so doing, they reckoned without allotting sufficient attention to such Goldwater Democrats as Lester G. Maddox.

Democracy
and Mr. Maddox

The Goldwater campaign had upset the normal partisan voting patterns in Georgia, and its impact, appearances would indicate, left a lasting impression on the contours of state voting patterns. At first glance, the 1966 state elections appeared equally unique. For the first time in recent years, an Atlanta resident competed successfully for the Georgia governorship, and he did so by more ardently championing rural values than any competitor. A two-term Democratic congressman, already renominated by popular election, took the unprecedented step of withdrawing from the campaign to protest the principles espoused by the Democratic nominee for governor. A Republican won a plurality in the gubernatorial election. Although more people cast ballots in the 1966 general election than had ever done before in a Georgia gubernatorial contest, the state legislature eventually selected the state chief executive. The voters overwhelmingly rejected progressivism at the very time that reapportionment, the rise of two-party competition, and the 1965 voting rights law were supposed to be contributing to the liberalization of politics. Nevertheless, traditional political divisions lay firmly at the base of the political warfare of 1966.

The Democratic gubernatorial primary election offered voters an unusually wide range of choices.[1] Lester G. Maddox, the urban advocate of rural values, clearly occupied the position furthest to the ideological right. James Gray and Garland T. Byrd were in the Bourbon Democratic tradition. Jimmy Carter, state senator from Sumter County, projected a moderately progressive image. Ellis G. Arnall, past leader of the anti-Talmadge faction, came closest to occupying a liberal position.[2] Table 5-1 shows the percentage of votes received by the major candidates by county groups.

Ideologically, Lester Maddox was reminiscent of Eugene Talmadge, who had won his last election 20 years previously. Like "Ol' Gene," Maddox fervently championed honesty and morality in government, segregation in social relationships, fundamentalism in religion, and the sanctity of private property and free enterprise in economics.[3] He often publicly associated social and ideological change with socialism, communism, and atheism. Born poor, he prospered in the restaurant business. In 1957 and again in 1961 he campaigned unsuccessfully for the mayor's office in Atlanta. During the early 1960's, he was a spokesman for the extreme segregationists who opposed public school desegregation, the sit-in movement, and other civil rights activities. In 1962 he entered the Democratic primary for lieutenant governor and won sufficient votes to squeeze into a runoff campaign against Peter Zack Geer,

---

[1] The following discussion of the candidates and issues in the 1966 elections in Georgia is based upon: (1) Bruce Galphin's perceptive work, *The Riddle of Lester Maddox;* (2) the Atlanta *Constitution* and the Atlanta *Journal* and, to a lesser extent, the Macon *Telegraph* and the Macon *News;* and (3) the author's personal observations (the author was a resident of Atlanta during the period and worked in a volunteer capacity for one of the candidates).

[2] A sixth candidate, Hoke O'Kelley, was a perennial contender who enjoyed talking about the Civil War and otherwise apparently relished campaigning. He received a negligible share of the vote.

[3] On Eugene Talmadge, see Lemmon, "The Ideology of Eugene Talmadge," 226-48; on Maddox, see Galphin, *Riddle of Lester Maddox.*

Table 5-1

Percentage of Votes Received by Democratic Gubernatorial Contenders in the 1966
  Primary Election

Candidate	South (rural) (town)	Black Belt (rural) (town)	North (rural) (town)	14 Urban Cos.	Fulton Co. (Atl.)	Total Vote
Maddox	33.2 (35.7) (30.2)	21.7 (22.8) (16.2)	27.9 (30.9) (24.3)	18.1	18.9	23.6
Gray-Byrd	31.1 (32.3) (29.7)	35.0 (34.5) (37.3)	19.1 (20.4) (17.5)	24.5	12.1	24.5*
Carter	12.8 (10.2) (15.9)	15.6 (15.0) (18.5)	25.3 (23.1) (27.8)	24.2	22.5	20.9
Arnall	21.0 (19.4) (22.7)	26.1 (26.0) (26.7)	25.5 (22.3) (29.3)	31.8	45.3	29.4

Totals do not equal 100 percent because of a sixth minor candidate.

*Gray finished fourth behind Arnall, Maddox, and Carter with 19.4 percent of the vote; Byrd came in a poor fifth.

an extreme conservative and the favorite in the race. Maddox was relatively unknown in south and central Georgia, areas that went heavily for Geer. Maddox ran surprisingly well in the Atlanta area and in north Georgia, however, and again, as he had done in his mayoralty races, he demonstrated a charismatic appeal to lower status white voters. During the early the early 1960's, he resisted all efforts to desegregate his flourishing Pickrick restaurant, brandishing a pistol on one occasion to drive away unwanted Negro customers. Ultimately he closed the Pickrick rather than comply with the public accommodations section of the 1964 civil rights law. By 1966 Maddox's reputation as a segregationist par excellence was well established, as was his image as an "irresponsible" white supremacy fanatic. Maddox attracted almost no endorsements from established politicians, and compared to most of the other major contenders, his campaign was pathetically financed and virtually devoid of organizational support.

Sharing the right side of the political spectrum with Maddox were James Gray and Garland Byrd. Both were associated with the Talmadge faction, and Gray came closer than any of the other candidates to wearing the Talmadge mantle in the campaign. Former Governor S. Ernest Vandiver, who withdrew early in the campaign because of a heart condition, was the original favorite of the Talmadge-oriented leadership in the state. Vandiver's withdrawal threw many of these politicians into panic. Most of Talmadge's political friends deemed only Vandiver capable of preventing the re-entry of Ellis Arnall into a prominent position in Democratic politics and of defeating the Republican threat headed by Congressman Bo Callaway, who was already conducting a well-financed and formidable challenge to the Democratic monopoly on the governor's office. Senator Talmadge himself publicly considered entering the campaign in order to turn back the Arnall–Callaway onslaught, but important financial interests in Georgia considered his presence and his seniority in the Senate too important to be sacrificed. Consequently, Gray and Byrd entered the race.

Gray, an Albany newspaper and television entrepreneur, was well educated and articulate—indeed, as Bruce Galphin has observed, "perhaps too polished for his 1966 constituency."[4] His campaign was adequately financed, and as past chairman of the state Democratic party, he was a political veteran who commanded substantial organizational support. In the 1964 presidential race, Gray had backed Goldwater's candidacy, and he endorsed many of the Arizona senator's conservative views. Gray promised to maintain law and order and to resist the programs of the "pampering federal government."[5]

Garland Byrd shared Gray's conservative outlook. A former lieutenant governor and once a power in Georgia politics, Byrd had sought the governorship in 1962 but had been forced to withdraw from the race because of ill health. In 1964 he campaigned for a seat in the House of Representatives from the Third Congressional District, only to be submerged by Bo Callaway and the Goldwater Republican tide. In 1966 most of the state's Democratic political and financial leadership joined with either Gray or Arnall, and Byrd's campaign, like that of Maddox's, was poorly financed and organized. Although he received too many votes to be ignored, Byrd was never a major contender, and in this discussion his votes have been combined with those for Gray.

[4] Galphin, *Riddle of Lester Maddox*, p. 110.
[5] As quoted in the Atlanta *Constitution*, August 3, 1966.

Maddox, Gray, and Byrd occupied the political and ideological right in the campaign, and they divided a majority of the votes cast in the traditionally conservative areas of the state. Together, they carried the south and central portions of the state and rural areas to the north. The votes they received correlated positively with the votes cast for past conservative alternatives. As Table 5-2 indicates, Gray and Byrd, who were residents of the Georgia lowlands, most closely associated with Senator Talmadge, and regarded as more "responsible" defenders of the status quo than Maddox, were in the mainstream of Georgia conservatism.

Table 5-2

Correlations between the Votes for Maddox and Gray–Byrd and the Conservative Vote in Selected State Elections

	Maddox	Gray–Byrd
Talmadge, 1946	.5182	.8669
Talmadge, 1948	.6114	.8028
Talmadge, 1950	.6703	.7118
Pro County Unit, 1952	.7247	.7078
Pro Private Schools, 1954	.6642	.7360
Griffin-Linder, 1954	.6955	.6353
Pro "Free" Electors, 1960	.2220	.8851
Griffin, 1962	.3753	.8966
Goldwater, 1964	.0087	.9252

Jimmy Carter occupied a moderately progressive position. Although little known outside his home bailiwick in the southwestern black belt, he projected a favorable image and conducted a well-financed, keep-Georgia-moving–type campaign that some felt resembled the 1960 Kennedy presidential campaign. He ran best in north Georgia and in the urban areas; his campaign fared most poorly in his native lowlands.

Competing with Carter for the anti-Talmadge vote was Ellis G. Arnall. Entering politics in the 1930's, Arnall served as attorney general and in 1943–47 was governor. His tenure in the governor's office was the most progressive and probably the most effective in modern Georgia history. The Talmadge faction's domination of Georgia Democratic politics during the mid-1950's forced Arnall into political inactivity. He publicly reappeared during the school desegregation controversy in the early 1960's, threatening to enter the 1962 gubernatorial race if Governor Vandiver and his advisors carried through their threat to close the public schools to prevent desegregation. When the schools were not closed, Arnall bided his time until the 1966 race. Arnall created an extensive campaign organization, and his effort was amply financed. But he had not competed for public office since 1942, and as Galphin phrased it, "the oratorical style that wowed 'em when he beat ol' Gene Talmadge sounded like a parody on TV."[6] Arnall's platform was more progressive than that of any of the other candidates. Despite the economic and demographic changes that had taken place in the state, Arnall appealed most strongly to voters residing in the same areas that had supported the anti-Talmadge faction 20 years before.

Table 5-3

Correlations between the Votes for Arnall and Carter and the Progressive Vote in Selected Elections by County Voter Categories

	Arnall	Carter
Carmichael, 1946	.9336	.7450
Thompson, 1948	.9359	.7351
Thompson, 1950	.9560	.6635
Against County Unit, 1952	.8533	.8439
Against Private Schools, 1954	.8227	.8407
Thompson–Gowen, 1954	.5661	.4514
For Pledged Electors, 1960	.6997	.6397
Sanders, 1962	.8390	.6957
Johnson, 1964	.4941	.7316

In the cities Arnall swept the black precincts and ran well among the more affluent whites. He was clearly the coalition candidate in both Atlanta and Macon. Maddox, Gray, and Byrd split the anticoalition vote. Although running best in more affluent white areas, Carter's personal appeal served him well among white voters generally. Table 5-4 compares the votes received by the Democratic gubernatorial aspirants and the votes cast in selected previous elections.

Arnall finished first in the balloting, but his 29.4 percent of the vote was an unimpressive showing for the candidate widely

[6] Galphin, *Riddle of Lester Maddox*, p. 110.

Table 5-4

Correlations between the Votes for Maddox, Gray-Byrd, Carter, and Arnall and the Conservative Vote in Selected Elections in Atlanta and Macon

	Maddox	Gray-Byrd	Carter	Arnall
Talmadge, 1948				
Macon	.9169	.9460	.6471	-.9471
Talmadge, 1950				
Macon	.9336	.9522	.6339	-.9527
Pro County Unit, 1952				
Atlanta	.9589	.8142	.5001	-.8882
Macon	.8965	.9344	.6133	-.9249
Pro Private Schools, 1954				
Atlanta	.9824	.8887	.6632	-.9714
Macon	.8924	.9608	.6761	-.9524
Maddox (Mayoralty runoff), 1961				
Atlanta	.9324	.9211	.6306	-.9328
Griffin, 1962				
Atlanta	.9633	.9268	.6423	-.9576
Macon	.9754	.9738	.6086	-.9670
Vickers (Aldermanic runoff), 1965				
Atlanta	.9262	.9573	.7231	-.9702
Geer (Lt. Governor runoff primary), 1966				
Atlanta	.9683	.9003	.6319	-.9521
Macon	.9813	.9587	.5995	-.9624

regarded as the favorite in the race. Maddox finished second (to the surprise of many observers who found it difficult to take him seriously) and thus qualified as Arnall's opponent in the runoff election. Again Arnall failed to spark popular enthusiasm, while Maddox fueled his campaign with fundamentalist fervor and a certain charisma. In the runoff primary election Maddox ran well ahead of other conservative candidates. Tables 5-5 and 5-6 compare the vote received by Maddox with the tallies in the Fifth Congressional District Democratic primary and in the runoff primary for lieutenant governor. Charles Weltner, who was nominated in the first primary, was of generally the same political persuasion as Arnall. Wyman C. Lowe was his chief opponent. Although Lowe was a noticeably poor campaigner and possessed little discernible financial or organizational support, he nevertheless ran ahead of Weltner in four of the five categories of white voters. In the lieutenant governor's race, George T. Smith was to the right of both Arnall and Weltner, but he was relatively "moderate" in comparison to Peter Zack Geer, the incumbent who had defeated Maddox four years before. Smith's folksy, common-man campaign style and his less progressive image gave him an appeal to rural and lower income white voters that Arnall and Weltner did not possess. Thus, in Tables 5–5 and 5–6, Lowe, Geer, and Maddox occupied the conservative positions. For comparative purposes, additionally, the combined vote for Maddox, Gray, and Byrd in the first primary is included.

Table 5–5

Percentage of Votes Received by Conservative Candidates in Selected 1966 Democratic Primary Elections in Georgia

Candidate	South (rural) (town)	Black Belt (rural) (town)	North (rural) (town)	14 Urban Cos.	Fulton Co. (Atl.)
Maddox–Gray–Byrd (combined vote)	64.3 (68.0) (59.9)	56.7 (57.3) (53.5)	47.0 (51.3) (41.8)	42.6	31.0
Geer	55.6 (61.5) (48.9)	51.4 (52.4) (46.8)	48.6 (52.1) (44.4)	40.8	27.0
Maddox	69.4 (72.7) (65.5)	61.4 (62.0) (58.6)	60.5 (65.8) (54.2)	48.2	35.0

Maddox won something over 54 percent of the popular vote. He swept the rural and small town areas of the state and handily carried the nonaffluent precincts in the cities. Arnall was left with the votes of Negroes and affluent whites, who provided him with sufficient votes to win majorities in the cities but not the state. Maddox, in addition to running ahead of other conservative candidates, drew a greater percentage of votes in the runoff primary than he, Gray, and Byrd together had been able to attract in the first primary. Since Carter's campaign had to a considerable extent rested upon the projection of a favorable image and an attractive personality, he no doubt won support from voters who were not necessarily oriented toward progressivism. These voters presumably shifted to Maddox in the second primary. Some lower echelon G.O.P. elements mounted a minor campaign to encourage

Table 5-6

Percentage of Votes Received by Conservative Candidates in Selected 1966 Democratic Primary Elections in Atlanta and Macon

Candidate	Poor White	Working Class White	Middle Income White	Semi-Affluent White	Affluent White	Black Poor	Black Nonpoor
Atlanta							
Maddox–Gray–							
Byrd	62.4	55.0	49.5	36.9	27.3	4.5	4.1
Lowe	50.4	49.9	50.1	46.2	32.5	2.5	3.5*
Geer	47.5	45.9	42.1	37.9	22.1	8.3	6.0
Maddox	73.5	67.5	61.7	51.9	31.1	1.7	1.0
Macon							
Maddox–Gray–							
Byrd	62.4	64.3	61.7	61.6	42.5		9.5
Geer	52.0	55.3	50.8	54.3	39.5		21.4
Maddox	68.5	73.2	69.3	67.8	42.2		7.2

*A third minor candidate shared the vote with Lowe and Weltner. Weltner's totals (in the same order as Lowe's) were: 36.8, 37.5, 40.3, 45.1, 59.7, 94.3, 93.9.

Republicans to vote for Maddox on the mistaken assumption that he would be easier to defeat in the general election than Arnall. The statistics clearly suggest that some voters who opted for Maddox in the runoff primary joined with Callaway in the general election (compare the Maddox vote in Tables 5-5 and 5-6 with that in Tables 5-7 and 5-8). It is doubtful, however, that a purposive Republican cross-over vote had much effect on the outcome of the election. More probable is the supposition that numerous conservative voters preferred Maddox to Arnall but ultimately favored the more "respectable" conservatism of Bo Callaway.

Republicans awaited the 1966 general election with scarcely restrained optimism. Goldwater had carried the state in 1964. Republican candidates had registered several impressive victories in the 1965 special state legislative elections, winning every seat in the Bibb County (Macon) delegation. The G.O.P. opened its 1966 drive by sweeping the city elections in Savannah in early August. Conservative Republicans won the mayor's office and all six aldermanic positions in Georgia's second largest city. By the time of Maddox's runoff victory, Callaway's lavishly financed and meticulously organized gubernatorial campaign was well underway. To grasp Callaway's coattails at the time of his expected victory, the G.O.P. entered congressional candidates in eight of Georgia's ten districts.

Originally a Democrat, Callaway had associated with the Talmadge faction during the 1950's. In 1962 he supported Griffin in his gubernatorial campaign against Sanders. Callaway shifted to Republicanism in 1964 and capitalized on Goldwater's popularity in the central part of the state to win the Third District congressional seat. As a member of the House, Callaway established a voting record that some sources rated the most conservative in the Georgia congressional delegation, a feat of no mean magnitude considering the ideological orientation of the Georgia congressional delegation.[7] "God, the individual, and free enterprise," Callaway stated, were the governmental concepts for which he stood.[8] In the gubernatorial campaign, Callaway never strayed from the conservative stance that had carried the cities and the south and central Georgia lowlands for Goldwater in 1964 and, indeed, had won for Callaway his congressional seat.

Maddox, now the nominee of the Georgia Democratic party, benefited from far greater organizational assistance than he had possessed in his two primary campaigns. Generally, the Democratic officials in the county courthouses throughout the countryside aided the Maddox effort, and, reportedly, Senator Talmadge quietly used his influence to muster support for the Democratic cause.[9] Maddox's campaign resources remained relatively meager in comparison to those available to Callaway, however.

Faced with a choice between Maddox and Callaway, liberal-progressive citizens organized a write-in movement in support of Arnall. Although Arnall did not publicly endorse the effort on his behalf, he also did not repudiate it. The write-in campaign spread across the state and enjoyed considerable support among black

[7] For example, Callaway was the only Georgia member of the 89th Congress to be assigned a "liberal" rating of "0" by the Americans for Democratic Action. *ADA World*, November, 1966.

[8] As quoted by Reuben Smith, in the Atlanta *Constitution*, September 20, 1966.

[9] Arlie Schardt, "Georgia: Lester Maddox and the Mad Democrats," *Reporter* 35 (October 20, 1966): 29-30.

voters. The results of the 1966 general election for governor are shown in Tables 5-7 and 5-8.

Table 5-7

Percentage of Votes Received by Candidates for Governor in the 1966 General Election in Georgia

Candidate	South (rural)(town)	Black Belt (rural)(town)	North (rural)(town)	14 Urban Cos.	Fulton County (Atl.)	Total
Callaway	33.0 (28.0) (38.9)	38.0 (36.4) (44.7)	35.5 (32.0) (39.9)	57.9	58.7	46.5
Maddox	62.8 (68.3) (56.5)	53.6 (54.5) (49.6)	60.3 (65.2) (54.2)	34.3	28.3	46.2
Write-in	4.2 (3.7) (4.6)	8.4 (9.0) (5.7)	4.2 (2.8)(5.9)	7.8	12.9	7.3

Table 5-8

Percentage of Votes Received by Candidates for Governor in the 1966 General Election in Atlanta and Macon

Atlanta	Poor White	Working Class White	Middle Income White	Semi-Affluent White	Affluent White	Black Poor	Black Nonpoor
Callaway	23.1	39.8	42.9	58.5	79.5	49.1	53.5
Maddox	72.2	56.1	51.7	36.8	12.5	2.8	3.4
Write-in	4.7	4.1	5.3	4.7	8.0	48.2	43.2
Macon*							
Callaway	52.6	47.9	47.0	55.2	77.8	87.4	
Maddox	47.4	52.1	53.0	44.8	22.2	12.6	

*Reported returns in Macon did not include write-in totals.

Callaway ran extremely well in the cities. He swept the affluent white neighborhoods, won a majority of the semi-affluent white votes, and made respectable showings in all of the lower status white categories except the poor white class in Atlanta. He was also the beneficiary of a significant anti-Maddox vote on the part of black voters. The countryside belonged to Maddox, although Callaway did far better in the counties containing larger towns than he did in rural areas. Callaway's approximately 121,000-vote edge over Maddox in the urban areas narrowly offset Maddox's 118,000 plurality in the countryside to give the Republican a slight plurality of the popular vote. The write-in movement denied either candidate a majority by attracting something over 7 percent of the vote (actually more since many write-in ballots were disqualified on technical grounds). With no candidate receiving a majority, the predominately Democratic state legislature chose Maddox as governor.

Maddox required assistance from the write-in campaign and the state legislature to become governor, but his 1966 performance at the polls was nevertheless impressive. He emerged victorious over two heavily favored opponents, both of whom possessed greater financial and organizational support than had been available to him. Maddox failed to win the decisive majorities among lower status white voters in urban areas that would have limited Callaway's majorities in the cities. Consequently, he finished second in the balloting, winning 46.2 percent of the vote, compared to Callaway's 46.5 percent. Maddox substantially held together the conservative voting coalition in the state, however, despite the Goldwater-type campaign strategy employed by Callaway. Table 5-9 compares Maddox's votes in the runoff primary and the general election with the conservative votes in a number of previous contests.

Republican congressional candidates based their campaign on linking their Democratic opponents to the Great Society programs of the Johnson Administration. Given the voting records of most of the Georgia House delegation and with Lester Maddox heading the Democratic ticket, the Republican campaign faced understandable difficulties. In Macon, G. Paul Jones, Jr., the Republican nominee, could hardly denounce his arch-conservative incumbent opponent, John H. Flynt, for the heresy of liberalism. Consequently, Jones attacked Flynt's record for being "far behind" the conservative position of two other Georgia congressmen.[10] Only in the Atlanta area did Republicans have some grounds for associating the opposition with the liberal policies of the national Democratic party. Fletcher M. Thompson, the G.O.P. candidate in the Fifth District, was successful in his campaign against Archie Lindsey. Charles Weltner, the incumbent, had defeated Wyman Lowe in the Fifth District Democratic primary. When Maddox

[10] Art Pine, in the Atlanta *Constitution*, August 4, 1966.

Table 5-9

Correlations between the Votes for Maddox in the 1966 Democratic Runoff Primary and in the General Election and the Conservative Votes in Selected Elections in Georgia, Atlanta, and Macon

	Maddox: Runoff			Maddox: General Election		
	Georgia	Atlanta	Macon	Georgia	Atlanta	Macon
Maddox—runoff, 1966	——	——	——	.9473	.9633	.9568
Geer—runoff, 1966	.9748	.9971	.9944	.9202	.9614	.9357
Lowe—primary, 1966	——	.9787	——	——	.8916	——
Against Liquor by the Drink—1964	——	.9335	——	——	.9374	——
Griffin—primary, 1962	.8620	.9951	.9965	.7589	.9627	.9456
Kennedy—1960	.8978	.9415	.2323*	.9078	.9605	.4679*
Stevenson—1956	.8684	.9638	.9736	.8249	.8850	.9434
Pro Private Schools —1954	.8970	.9867	.9473	.8357	.9468	.8734
Pro County Unit —1952	.9242	.9278	.9396	.8513	.9451	.8840
Talmadge—primary, 1950	.9532	——	.9674	.8557	——	.9024
Talmadge—primary, 1948	.9711	——	.9549	.8646	——	.8870

*The low correlations between Kennedy and Maddox in Macon reflect the fact that Negroes voted heavily for Kennedy.

became the Democratic gubernatorial nominee, Weltner withdrew from the race, explaining that he could not in principle honor the state Democratic party loyalty oath that bound all Democratic candidates to support the nominees of the party. The Fifth District Democratic executive committee chose Lindsey, chairman of the Fulton County Commission, as the new Democratic nominee. Lindsey took a relatively progressive stance in the brief period of campaign time that he had available. Thus Jones and Flynt both took extremely conservative positions, and Thompson was clearly to the right of Lindsey. Table 5-10 records the votes received by the two Republican candidates in Atlanta and Macon.

The class appeal of the Republican congressional candidate in Atlanta is readily apparent. Like Callaway, Thompson ran best

Table 5-10

Percentage of Votes Received by Republican Congressional Candidates in 1966 in Atlanta and Macon

Atlanta	Poor White	Working Class White	Middle Income White	Semi-Affluent White	Affluent White	Black Poor	Black Nonpoor
Thompson	35.1	53.0	53.2	68.2	72.1	32.7	30.2
Macon							
Jones	44.5	50.5	43.0	52.0	50.7		35.6

among the more affluent white voters. Thompson's modest showing in Atlanta's poor white neighborhoods was obviously related to the fact that Maddox carried 72 percent of the votes in the same precincts. Significantly, however, Republican congressional candidates ran well among urban whites generally. Jones carried three of five categories of white voters in Macon as white voters in the city divided about evenly. Flynt won Bibb County by taking a solid majority in black precincts. Thompson won a substantial majority of the votes of Atlanta's white citizens. Not unexpectedly, Maddox was a considerable liability for Democratic congressional candidates in urban areas. Without Maddox at the head of the Democratic column, it is highly doubtful that Thompson could have received more than 30 percent of the vote from black precincts. In the countryside, Maddox was an asset to Democratic aspirants. Republican congressional contenders ran feebly in nonurban areas.

Perhaps the most significant feature of the 1966 elections was the growing isolation of Negro voters. The central thrust of Negro political activity in the gubernatorial campaign was toward the write-in movement. Despite the difficulties involved in casting a write-in vote, approximately 45 percent of Atlanta's black voters opted for Arnall. With both of the major party candidates effectively writing off Negro voters, substantial numbers of Negroes throughout the state reacted by grasping a third-party alternative. In Atlanta two-thirds of the voters in black precincts voted for Lindsey, while four of five categories of white voters delivered majorities to Thompson. Macon Negroes remained in the Democratic fold in the Sixth Congressional District, although Flynt shared with Jones a belligerently hostile attitude toward civil rights progress. In the city elections in Savannah earlier in the year, Republican candidates had carried every white precinct in the city and had won a reported three percent of the ballots from black precincts.[11]

Maddox captured the governorship, and all but two of the Democratic congressional candidates turned back the Republican challenge. Conservative Republicans replaced Weltner and James A. Mackay, the only two progressive members of the Georgia congressional delegation. The still-emerging Negro vote was effectively isolated. Similar voting patterns were to appear during the 1968 elections in Georgia.

[11] Atlanta *Constitution*, August 5, 8, 1966.

The 1968 Elections

In 1948, J. Strom Thurmond ran for president of the United States on the third-party Dixiecrat ticket and won approximately 20 percent of the popular vote in Georgia. Two decades later another Deep South segregationist running as a third-party candidate won a plurality in Georgia with 43 percent of the popular vote. It is true that George C. Wallace's campaign in Georgia was more effective than Thurmond's. But more basically, Wallace's success reflected the deterioration of the national Democratic party's position in the state and the heightened social and ideological fears of traditionalist white voters.

The 1968 presidential election etched the basic divisions in Georgia politics more clearly than any recent political contest. Appealing to white rural voters and to lower status whites in the cities, Wallace won a majority of the ballots cast by white Georgians. Richard M. Nixon was the candidate of the urban bourgeoisie, but he was also Wallace's chief competitor among white voters generally. Nixon finished second in the balloting with approximately 30 percent of the vote. Black voters formed the base of Hubert H. Humphrey's following. Humphrey won just under 27 percent of the vote to run last in the three-cornered contest. Tables 6-1 and 6-2 show the returns in Georgia, Atlanta, and Macon.

Table 6-1

Percentage of Votes Received by Presidential Candidates in the 1968 Election in Georgia

Candidate	South (rural) (town)	Black Belt (rural) (town)	North (rural) (town)	14 Urban Cos.	Fulton Co. (Atl.)
Wallace	60.4 (64.3) (54.2)	50.6 (49.6) (55.2)	51.5 (52.9) (49.7)	35.8	20.7
Nixon	20.1 (18.1) (22.7)	19.8 (20.0) (19.1)	28.1 (28.0) (28.1)	38.6	35.7
Humphrey	19.6 (17.7) (23.0)	29.6 (30.4) (25.7)	20.4 (19.1) (22.2)	25.5	43.6

Table 6-2

Percentage of Votes Received by Presidential Candidates in the 1968 Election in Atlanta and Macon

Atlanta	Poor White	Working Class White	Middle Income White	Semi-Affluent White	Affluent White	Black Poor	Black Nonpoor
Wallace	54.8	42.2	43.5	33.9	11.9	0.6	0.5
Nixon	18.2	35.2	33.4	43.3	58.4	2.0	1.6
Humphrey	27.0	22.6	23.0	22.8	29.7	97.5	97.9
Macon							
Wallace	56.7	61.9	58.1	59.1	28.0	7.6	
Nixon	31.8	27.2	26.9	28.2	54.3	5.8	
Humphrey	11.5	10.9	15.1	12.7	17.6	86.6	

No doubt, the Wallace appeal in Georgia, as elsewhere in the nation, rested primarily on racism. Early in the campaign, Roy V. Harris, Wallace's Georgia campaign manager, observed: "When you get down to it, there's really going to be only one issue, and you spell it n-i-g-g-e-r."[1] The assassination of Dr. Martin Luther King, Jr., the subsequent rioting in a number of cities outside Georgia, and the massive attendance at King's funeral in Atlanta provided a campaign backdrop tinged with racial emotionaliam. The continuing controversy over public school desegregation and the school desegregation guidelines administered by the Department of Health, Education, and Welfare kept racial issues immediate in Georgia. In this atmosphere, Wallace's reputation as a defender of "segregation now, segregation tomorrow, segregation forever" appealed strongly to many Georgia whites.[2] The right of local white officials to control local schools without intervention by "bureaucrats" from the Health, Education, and Welfare Department ranked with "Americanism," "state's rights," and "law and order" as recurring themes in Wallace's Georgia campaign literature.

But Wallace's attraction rested on more than just negrophobia. In 1948 Thurmond had won only 10 percent of the vote in north Georgia, and even Goldwater had carried no better than 44.2 percent of the vote in the northern uplands. Against two major party opponents, however, Wallace won a majority of the ballots cast in the towns and counties of the north. Himself the product of a rural Alabama county, Wallace spoke the idiom of the countryside. He combined racism and a (white) common-man campaign style with a generai defense of rural–southern–small-town values. The Wallace campaign substantially rested on the assumption that folk customs and traditional modes of behavior were of more importance than laws, constitutional processes, and intellectual theories.[3] At the same time, Wallace appealed to the

---

[1] As quoted in Margaret Shannon, "The Next President's Georgia Campaign," Atlanta *Journal and Constitution Magazine*, November 3, 1968, p. 54. The following discussion of the 1968 presidential campaign in Georgia is based on: (1) Shannon, "The Next President's Georgia Campaign"; (2) the Atlanta *Constitution* and the Atlanta *Journal*; (3) the "State of the Southern States: Georgia" series in *New South* 23, 24 (Winter, 1968, to Spring, 1969); and (4) the author's personal observations (as in 1966, the author was a resident of Atlanta during 1968 and worked in one of the congressional campaigns).

[2] The quotation is from *The Inaugural Address of Governor George C. Wallace* (Montgomery: n.p., 1963), pp. 2–3.

[3] See Reese Cleghorn, *Radicalism Southern Style: A Commentary on Regional Extremism of the Right* (Atlanta: Southern Regional Council,

defensiveness felt by many Georgia traditionalists. Realizing that Nixon was his major opponent in Georgia, Wallace stated in his final campaign rally in Atlanta that the Republican party "has looked down their noses at every Georgian and every Alabaman and every Southerner for the last 100 years. They wouldn't spit on a Georgian except for your vote, but we have them shaken up."[4] Although Wallace himself rarely mentioned religion, his Georgia campaign workers distributed literature that included the Alabamian in "God's plan," a campaign strategy that may well have assisted Wallace in the northern part of the state.

Working for the Wallace cause in Georgia were such political veterans as Harris, former lieutenant governor Peter Zack Geer, and former governor Marvin Griffin. As an Atlanta journalist observed in reference to Harris' crude remark about the only campaign issue being spelled "n-i-g-g-e-r," "the enlistment of race experts like Marvin Griffin and Peter Zack Geer meant the Wallace team in Georgia had men who knew how to spell."[5] Governor Lester Maddox was another "race expert" who actively supported the Wallace cause. The American Independent party's Georgia campaign was a loosely organized but nevertheless vigorous effort that Harris described as "the damnedest grassroots movement you ever saw."[6]

Not surprisingly, Wallace was the clear choice of the conservative voting coalition in Georgia. The Independent party candidate overwhelmed the opposition in south Georgia, won a majority in the black belt and in the rural areas of north Georgia, and like Maddox in 1966, fared well in the north Georgia towns, where he won a substantial plurality. He outdistanced both of his opponents among the lower status voters in the cities. In Macon Wallace

---

1968), pp. 13-16, and Marshall Frady, *Wallace* (New York: World, 1968), pp. 1-48.

[4] As quoted in the Atlanta *Constitution*, November 5, 1968. Customary *sic's* have been omitted, since Wallace normally failed to bring nouns, verbs, and pronouns into agreement.

[5] Shannon, "The Next President's Georgia Campaign," p. 54. Griffin was the American Independent party's temporary vice presidential nominee, and his name appeared along with that of Wallace on most Georgia ballots despite the later nomination of General (USAF ret.) Curtis LeMay.

[6] As quoted in Shannon, "The Next President's Georgia Campaign," p. 54.

won a majority in every white voter category except the most affluent. In Atlanta he won a majority of the poor white votes and carried pluralities in working class and middle income precincts. As Table 6-3 indicates, the Wallace vote correlated significantly with the votes received by the conservative candidates in past elections.

Table 6-3

Correlations between the Vote for Wallace in the 1968 Presidential Election and the Conservative Votes in Selected Elections in Georgia, Atlanta, and Macon

| | Wallace | | |
	Georgia	Atlanta	Macon
Talmadge, 1948 gubernatorial	.9296	———	.9139
Talmadge, 1950 gubernatorial	.8748	———	.9327
For County Unit Amendment, 1952	.8475	.9313	.8994
Griffin-Linder, 1954 gubernatorial	.9732	———	.9107
For Private School Amendment, 1954	.8630	.9529	.8989
Stevenson, 1956 presidential	.8757	.9362	.9698
Kennedy, 1960 presidential	.9044	.9693	.3490
Maddox, 1961 runoff mayoralty	———	.9801	———
Griffin, 1962 gubernatorial	.8840	.9864	.9833
Against liquor by the drink, 1964	———	.9648	———
Vickers, aldermanic runoff, 1965	———	.9570	———
Geer, lieutenant governor runoff, 1966	.9389	.9817	.9845
Lowe, Fifth District runoff, 1966	———	.9337	———
Maddox, runoff gubernatorial, 1966	.9565	.9813	.9879
Maddox, general election, 1966	.9217	.9913	.9797
Against fluoridation, 1968	———	.9828	———

In the broadest sense, Wallace's success with the Georgia electorate reflected the same rejection of national ideals that had fueled the Goldwater appeal to Georgia voters. But the differences were also substantial. Wallace's appeal to the white common "folks" was not of the same ideological persuasion as Goldwater's business-oriented individualism. The correlation between the response of Georgia voter categories to Goldwater and Wallace was a relatively insignificant .5053. In the cities, the anti-civil-rights positions of both candidates attracted sufficient support from white voters generally and alienated Negro voters sufficiently to result in higher correlations. Among Atlanta voter categories, the Goldwater-Wallace correlation was .8086; in Macon it was .8633. This apparent relationship between the urban votes for the two candidates diminished when Negro votes were excluded. The correlation between Goldwater and Wallace based only on the response of white voters in Atlanta was .0752.

Richard Nixon competed with Wallace for the votes of white Georgians. The well-financed and closely organized Republican campaign cast the Nixon candidacy in an aura of conservatism. Georgia Republicans stressed Nixon's economically conservative positions on such topics as inflation and taxation and his socially conservative stands clothed in the terminology of patriotism and law and order. The G.O.P. sought to counter the Wallace appeal by insisting that the American Independent candidate could not win and that therefore a vote for Wallace was a vote wasted if not, effectively, a vote for Humphrey. While Georgia Republicans eschewed outright racism, Senator Thurmond of South Carolina spent three days in Georgia campaigning for the Republican presidential ticket, and Nixon spokesmen in the state included such Goldwater conservatives as Howard "Bo" Callaway, Nixon's southern campaign manager, and G. Paul Jones, Jr., of Macon, the Republican state chairman.

Nixon ran best in the cities. He won a majority of the votes of affluent whites in both Atlanta and Macon, and he carried a plurality of the votes of Atlanta's semi-affluent whites. The Republican candidate ran behind Wallace but ahead of Humphrey in every other category of white voters except the poor white group in Atlanta. Although he was unable to compete with Wallace in the countryside, Nixon won a greater number of nonurban votes than did Humphrey.

Georgia Republicans qualified a candidate to challenge Senator Herman E. Talmadge and three candidates for seats in the United States House of Representatives. Earl Patton, an Atlanta moderate, won 22.5 percent of the votes in his effort to unseat the entrenched and virtually unassailable Talmadge. Former Republican state chairman Joe Tribble campaigned unsuccessfully in the First Congressional District in the southeastern part of the state. Ben B. Blackburn and Fletcher Thompson, the two Republican incumbents, retained their House seats from the Atlanta area Fourth and Fifth Congressional Districts. Opposing Thompson and Blackburn were the former incumbents, Charles L. Weltner and James A. Mackay. Weltner had refused to seek a third term after

Maddox's nomination as governor in 1966, and Mackay, first elected to the House of Representatives in 1964, had been unseated by Blackburn in an extremely close election in 1966. As congressmen, Thompson and Blackburn had established ultraconservative voting records. In 1968 Blackburn stood on his record and attacked Mackay's "liberalism." Thompson projected a somewhat more moderate campaign image, but he nevertheless remained far to the right of Weltner. During the previous year in Macon, the Republicans had added the mayor's office to their list of conquests when Ronnie Thompson, a jewelry store owner and a gospel singer, defeated B. F. Merritt, Jr., the incumbent Democrat, to become the first G.O.P. mayor in Macon's history. The 1967 mayor's race in Macon was fought on local issues, although Thompson had on the eve of the election testily announced: "I must concede that the [Negro] bloc vote this time, as in the past, will go to my opponent, B. F. Merritt. . . ."[7]

Thompson's prediction proved to be quite correct; Negroes voted heavily for Merritt and for all the other major Democratic candidates. Conversely, however, Ronnie Thompson in Macon and Fletcher Thompson in Atlanta ran extremely well among lower status white voters. Fletcher Thompson was clearly the choice of voters who cast their ballots for either Wallace or Nixon. In Macon Ronnie Thompson's tallies in 1967 resembled Wallace's totals in 1968 and, among lower status white voters, virtually duplicated the 1964 Goldwater vote. The Republican candidates in both Atlanta and Macon appealed most successfully to the middle categories of white voters. Table 6–4 compares Fletcher Thompson's vote in Atlanta with the votes for Wallace and Nixon in 1968 and with the vote for Goldwater in 1964; it also records the 1964 Goldwater returns in Macon, the 1967 vote for Ronnie Thompson, and the 1968 Wallace vote.

Since 1964 the Republican party in Georgia has rarely deviated from the political strategy associated with the Goldwater candidacy. The occasional activities of such Atlanta moderates as senatorial candidate Earl Patton notwithstanding, the G.O.P. has sought to combine the economic conservatism and "good government" programs that have appealed to the more affluent urbanites

[7] As quoted in the Macon *News*, November 5, 1967.

Table 6-4

Percentage of Votes Received by Selected Candidates in Atlanta and Macon

Atlanta	Poor White	Working Class White	Middle Income White	Semi-Affluent White	Affluent White	Black Poor	Black Nonpoor
Wallace, 1968	54.8	42.2	43.5	33.9	11.9	0.6	0.5
Nixon, 1968	18.2	35.2	33.4	43.3	58.4	2.0	1.6
Thompson, 1968	63.4	72.8	74.3	74.8	65.7	3.2	2.9
Goldwater, 1964	57.6	56.5	62.5	62.4	57.4	1.2	0.6
Macon							
Wallace, 1968	56.7	61.9	58.1	59.1	28.0	7.6	
Thompson, 1967	65.5	73.7	68.8	75.7	38.3*	23.2	
Goldwater, 1964	68.3	74.8	68.8	73.5	67.7	13.6	

*Ronnie Thompson's poor showing in affluent white precincts was significant, but it also reflected, in part at least, a long-standing rivalry in Macon between the affluent neighborhoods in the northern part of the city and the middle income and semi-affluent Bloomfield–Godfrey section to the south and west. Thompson's vote in the mayoralty race correlated with the vote for George Wallace at a .9904 level.

with the social and ideological conservatism that has attracted the support of the lower status whites. The election successes of Fletcher Thompson in Atlanta and Ronnie Thompson in Macon, as well as the successful G.O.P. mayoralty campaigns in the cities of Columbus and East Point during 1968, appeared to be a partial vindication of the strategy. In all of these contests the Republican party was obviously the party of the white common man.

Table 6-5 examines the shifting base of Republican voter support in Georgia. During the 1950's, the G.O.P. presented the moderately conservative image personified by Dwight Eisenhower. In the 1956 presidential election, Eisenhower ran best among Negroes and affluent whites in the cities. The vote for Eisenhower in 1956 correlated highly with the votes received by Randolph Thrower in the 1956 Fifth District congressional race and by Richard Nixon in the 1960 presidential election. During the 1960's, the Republicans abandoned Negro voters in quest of a

Table 6-5

Correlations between Selected Republican Candidates and Eisenhower (1956) and Goldwater in Georgia, Atlanta, and Macon, and by White Voter Categories only in Atlanta

	Eisenhower, 1956				Goldwater, 1964			
	Georgia	Atlanta	White Atlanta*	Macon	Georgia	Atlanta	White Atlanta*	Macon
Eisenhower, 1956	—	—	—	—	-.5320	-.9506	-.5297	-.8700
Thrower, 1956	—	.9986	.9929	—	—	-.9395	-.4889	—
Nixon, 1960	.9537	.8962	.8914	.3420	-.3638	-.7371	-.1471	.1453
O'Callaghan, 1962	—	-.1432	.8996	—	—	.4324	-.1893	—
Goldwater, 1964	-.5320	-.9506	-.5297	-.8700	—	—	—	—
O'Callaghan, 1964	—	-.9418	-.2243	—	—	.9994	.9231	—
Thompson, 1966	—	-.5165	.6315	—	—	.7232	.2461	—
Jones, 1966	·	—	—	-.5477	—	—	—	.8501
Thompson, 1967	—	—	—	-.9438	—	—	—	.8271
Thompson, 1968	—	-.9460	-.3442	—	—	.9951	.6521	—
Callaway, 1966 (Maddox)	.8556	.3375	.7856	.9434	-.1788	-.0639	.0873	-.7822
Nixon, 1968 (Wallace)	.9347	-.6159	8156	-.3251	-.5828	.8232	.0257	.6830
Patton, 1968 (Talmadge)	.8735	.4681	.8989	-.6134	-.2181	-.1933	-.1257	.9035

*Correlations based on five categories of white voters with two Negro voter categories excluded.

91

more broadly based white following. Nixon had failed to carry the black precincts in Macon in 1960, and James O'Callaghan attracted limited support in black neighborhoods in his 1962 congressional campaign in Atlanta. The Goldwater candidacy was, of course, the culmination of the development of a "lily white" strategy. Goldwater appealed to white voters in the cities and in the southern Georgia countryside. The vote for Goldwater correlated negatively with that for Eisenhower in 1956. Not only did Goldwater win virtually no Negro support, he projected an essentially classless appeal to white voters and won roughly equal support from every white socio-economic category. The votes received by several Republican candidates in Macon and Atlanta since 1964 show a closer relationship to the ballots cast for Goldwater than to those cast for Eisenhower. The G.O.P. has to some extent become the "white man's party" in Georgia. The Republican leadership's "lily white" strategy, it should be made clear, has not been based on racial demagoguery. Indeed, the G.O.P. has enjoyed considerable success in maintaining the "respectability" of the party. The strategy instead has conformed rather closely to the political design outlined by Kevin P. Phillips in *The Emerging Republican Majority*.[8] Thus far, the success or failure of Republican campaign tactics has to a considerable degree depended upon the opposition. When Callaway in 1966 sought to duplicate Goldwater's campaign success, the Democrats made Maddox their nominee. Callaway won a small plurality only by being the beneficiary of anti-Maddox votes cast by Negroes toward whom Callaway had made no public overtures at all. In 1968 Wallace reaped many of the votes that Nixon's conservative image would have otherwise apparently attracted.[9] Such candidates as Maddox, Wallace, and Talmadge have been able to drive the G.O.P. from the countryside and to contain the Republican beachheads in lower status white neighborhoods in the cities. As Table 6–5 indicates, the Republican party has appealed to a shifting and an increasingly conservative constituency that has been substantially influenced by the nature of opposition counter-measures.

[8] Kevin P. Phillips, *The Emerging Republican Majority* (New Rochelle, N.Y.: Arlington House, 1969), especially pp. 187–289.

[9] This point is examined in chapter 7.

Hubert H. Humphrey's Georgia campaign dramatized the disintegration of the national Democratic party's position in the state. Humphrey received little assistance from state Democratic party sources, and the overall effort on his behalf suffered from a lack of organizational and financial support. When the Democratic National Convention in Chicago divided Georgia's seats between the regular Maddox delegation and a liberal challenge group, several members of the Maddox delegation walked out of the convention.[10] Shortly afterward, the Georgia state treasurer, the comptroller general, the commissioner of agriculture, and the chairman and another member of the public service commission resigned their membership in the Democratic party to become Republicans. Collectively known as the "capitol clique," the five new Republican converts were among the more powerful men in the Georgia state government. Governor Maddox actively supported Wallace. In 1964 Governor Sanders worked for the national ticket and his position as head of the state government and of the state Democratic party encouraged professional politicians to offer at least nominal support for Johnson's candidacy. In 1968 both the governor and the "capitol clique" opposed Humphrey, and any Democrat who supported the Democratic ticket could anticipate no accolades at court. Consequently, the leadership for Humphrey's inchoate Georgia effort included Carl Vinson, a retired and aging veteran congressman who served as honorary chairman; Dr. Samuel Williams, a civil rights spokesman and the chairman of the Atlanta Community Relations Commission; and E. T. Kehrer, southern director of the AFL-CIO civil rights division. The organization functioned mainly in urban black neighborhoods.

Democratic campaign difficulties accurately mirrored the weakness of the national party ticket among Georgia voters. Humphrey swept the black precincts and ran poorly elsewhere. He won a plurality in Fulton County by carrying almost 98 percent of the Negro vote. He received almost 30 percent of the votes cast in the black belt, which probably represents a fairly accurate assess-

[10] The challenge was based on the grounds that the regular delegation was chosen in an undemocratic fashion (it was appointed by Maddox and state party chairman James Gray, both of whom supported Goldwater in 1964) and that it denied black Democrats fair representation (seven of the 107 delegates and alternates were Negroes).

ment of the effective Negro voting strength in that area. Humphrey won approximately 20 percent of the votes in the north and south Georgia countryside, and he took just over 25 percent in the 14 other urban counties. In Macon Humphrey ran last in every category of white voters. In Atlanta he finished third in the three middle white groups, but he did run second behind Nixon among affluent white voters and second behind Wallace among poor whites.

The Humphrey campaign, in its almost exclusive reliance upon the black community for support, resembled the campaigns of Maynard H. Jackson and Charles Weltner. Jackson, an articulate young Atlanta lawyer, challenged Herman Talmadge in the Democratic senatorial primary. The first Negro to be a candidate in a statewide campaign since Reconstruction, Jackson conducted an ill-financed but energetic campaign. He concentrated his efforts on black and poorer white voters, hoping, he stated, for a "rebirth of populism in Georgia."[11] "Talmadge promised segregation as a reward for your poverty, pain, and suffering," Jackson reiterated before lower status white audiences, "and he can't even deliver that."[12] Weltner once again defeated Wyman C. Lowe to win the Democratic nomination in the Fifth Congressional District. In the general election, Weltner ran as a progressive candidate against the staunchly conservative Republican incumbent. Table 6-6 compares the statewide vote for Humphrey and Jackson. Table 6-7 records the returns in Atlanta for Weltner, Jackson, and Humphrey and the votes in Macon for Jackson, Humphrey, and Democratic mayoralty candidate B. F. Merritt. All the candidates listed in Tables 6-6 and 6-7 were politically to the left of their opponents, and with the exception of Weltner's primary victory, all were defeated.

Both Jackson and Humphrey ran best in the cities, and both did better in the black belt than elsewhere in the countryside. In Atlanta and Macon the progressive candidates generally ran poorly in white areas. Since proportionately fewer whites voted in the

[11] As quoted in Paul Wieck, "No Love Lost," *New Republic* 159 (August 31, 1968): 10–11.

[12] As quoted in "State of the Southern States: Georgia," *New South* 23 (Summer, 1968): 69. See also Marvin Wall and Clarence Seeliger, "Post-Mortem of a Georgia Primary," *New South* 24 (Summer, 1969): 80–88.

Table 6-6

Percentage of Votes Received by Jackson and Humphrey in 1968 in Georgia

Candidate	South (rural) (town)	Black Belt (rural) (town)	North (rural) (town)	14 Urban Cos.	Fulton Co. (Atl.)
Jackson	16.2 (14.4) (18.6)	24.4 (24.4) (24.0)	12.2 (9.9) (15.4)	26.7	46.4
Humphrey	19.6 (17.7) (23.0)	29.6 (30.4) (25.7)	20.4 (19.1) (22.2)	25.5	43.6

Table 6-7

Percentage of Votes Received by Selected Candidates in 1967 and 1968 in Atlanta and Macon

Atlanta	Poor White	Working Class White	Middle Income White	Semi-Affluent White	Affluent White	Black Poor	Nonpoor
Weltner (Primary)	42.8	44.0	39.4	45.0	65.3	94.7	96.0
Weltner	36.6	27.2	25.7	25.2	34.3	96.8	97.1
Jackson	17.7	16.6	16.7	16.6	32.5	97.9	98.3
Humphrey	27.0	22.6	23.0	22.8	29.7	97.5	97.9
Macon							
Merritt	34.5	26.3	31.2	24.3	61.7	76.8	
Jackson	6.4	9.8	13.0	12.3	11.4	86.1	
Humphrey	11.5	10.9	15.1	12.7	17.6	86.6	

primary than in the general election, Jackson won a higher percentage of the vote in Fulton County than Humphrey did despite Humphrey's somewhat stronger showing in lower status white categories. The results of the Fifth District primary election and the Macon mayoralty race indicated that the Negro–affluent-white coalition was not dead. Both Weltner and Merritt won solid majorities in upper status white neighborhoods and in black communities. In Macon the votes of affluent whites and Negroes were not sufficient to overcome Ronnie Thompson's massive support among lower status whites. In the Fifth District general election, affluent whites shifted to Republicanism, and Weltner, like Humphrey and Jackson, ran well only among the black minority.

The successive returns in Fifth District elections during the 1960's suggested the increasing isolation of Negro voters in partisan politics. In 1962 and 1964, Weltner opposed conservative Republican James O'Callaghan. In 1966 Weltner's withdrawal led to Archie Lindsey's nomination as Fletcher Thompson's opponent. In 1968, of course, Weltner, who had grown more liberal during his years in and out of office, sought to regain the congressional seat from Thompson. Table 6-8 records the Democratic vote in each election.

Table 6-8

Percentage of Votes Received by Democratic Congressional Candidates in Atlanta

Atlanta	Poor White	Working Class White	Middle Income White	Semi-Affluent White	Affluent White	Black Poor	Black Nonpoor
Weltner, 1962	67.4	66.3	64.0	61.6	40.5	70.3	68.3
Weltner, 1964	44.6	43.1	38.2	37.7	41.8	98.5	98.8
Lindsey, 1966	64.9	47.0	46.8	31.8	27.9	67.3	69.8
Weltner, 1968	36.6	27.2	25.7	25.2	34.3	96.8	97.1

The decrease in Democratic support among Fifth District white voters was consistent with the general shift of the national Democratic party's voter base in Georgia from the conservative whites in the countryside and the lower status white districts in the cities to the black neighborhoods. The votes won by Humphrey bore little resemblance to those that provided the majorities for Stevenson and Kennedy in previous elections. Nor did the Humphrey vote bear any similarity to the vote for such state's rights Democrats as James C. Davis in his Fifth District victory over Republican Randolph Thrower or Lester Maddox in his successful endeavor against Callaway. Instead, Humphrey's vote correlated almost perfectly with the write-in vote in the 1966 gubernatorial election. Table 6-9 shows the coefficients of correlation between Humphrey's vote and the returns for other Democratic candidates in partisan elections.

The 1969 Atlanta city elections demonstrated that the polarization of voters along racial lines was not confined to partisan politics. Black and white voters split sharply in the principal con-

Table 6-9

Correlations between the Vote for Humphrey in the 1968 Presidential Election and the Votes for Selected Democratic Candidates in Georgia, Atlanta, and Macon

| | *Humphrey* | | |
	Georgia	Atlanta	Macon
Stevenson, 1956	-.5612	-.9527	-.8890
Davis, 1956	——	-.9447	——
Kennedy, 1960	-.6411	-.7627	.1071
Weltner, 1962	——	.3993	——
Johnson, 1964	.2847	.9969	.9954
Weltner, 1964	——	.9966	——
Lindsey, 1966	——	.7038	——
Merritt, 1967	——	——	.8183
Weltner, 1968	——	.9972	——
Maddox, 1966	-.8112	-.7686	-.7883

tests. The city elections resulted in a major break-through by black voters, whose candidates won the major offices. These candidates, however, recorded their victories without the support of affluent whites. The breakdown of the black–affluent-white coalition was the most significant result of the 1969 elections in Atlanta.

Four major candidates competed for the office being vacated by outgoing Mayor Ivan Allen, who chose not to seek a third term.[13] The contenders in this election, as well as those competing for other Atlanta offices, maintained relatively high standards in their campaigns, and the contests (with one partial and rather unusual exception) were unmarred by race-baiting, antics, and demagoguery. Within this context, Alderman G. Everett Millican easily qualified as the most conservative of the mayoralty contenders. He frequently spoke in defense of "law and order" and attacked the Atlanta "hippie" community, which had been the subject of a long-standing controversy involving the civil liberties of nonconformists and the scope of police authority in the enforcement of antidrug laws. Millican's campaign evidenced inadequate financial support, however, and at the age of 72, he found himself competing against three much younger and—at least in terms of the candidates' images—more vigorous opponents.

[13] Two minor candidates received a negligible share of the total vote. This discussion of the Atlanta elections is based on the Atlanta *Constitution* and the Atlanta *Journal*, August 1 to October 23, 1969.

Alderman Rodney M. Cook and Dr. Horace E. Tate shared the middle position in the mayoralty campaign. Cook was clearly the "establishment" candidate, the favorite of Mayor Allen and much of the Atlanta "power structure."[14] In his well-financed campaign, Cook took a progressive position on major issues and portrayed himself as the legitimate heir to the Allen administration. His campaign slogan was "Atlanta Needs Another Great Mayor." Although the election was nonpartisan, Cook was a member of the Republican party and had successfully campaigned under the G.O.P. banner in state legislative races. Tate, a member of the Atlanta board of education, an officer in the state Negro teachers' organization, and the holder of a Ph.D. in education, also projected a progressive image. A Negro, Tate, rather than his white opponents, made race an issue by stressing his blackness in Negro communities. Early in the campaign some Negro leaders suggested it was too early for a black candidate to win the mayor's office since something over 60 percent of the names on the registration rolls belonged to white people. Tate answered with the slogan "Brother Tate for Mayor Now This Time." He received endorsements from most of Atlanta's black civil-rights–oriented leaders, including Mrs. Coretta King, Dr. Ralph D. Abernathy, and Julian Bond.[15] Tate's campaign suffered, however, from lack of adequate financial support.

Vice Mayor Sam Massell, Jr., occupied a position to the left of his opponents. Jewish in religion and a self-proclaimed "liberal Democrat" in politics, Massell ran a vigorous campaign that was second only to that of Cook in the extent of its financial resources.[16] For eight years Massell had served as Ivan Allen's vice mayor, and he, like Cook, publicly identified himself with the accomplishments of the outgoing administration. Negro political leaders and a number of prominent labor union officials supported Massell in the campaign. The results of the election are shown in Table 6–10.

[14] See Jennings, *Community Influentials*, pp. 130–40.

[15] Most black political leaders in Atlanta supported Vice Mayor Sam Massell in the campaign.

[16] In Atlanta virtually all serious campaigns are handled by professional political consultative agencies. The one that "managed" Massell's effort is generally regarded as the most effective.

Table 6-10

Percentage of Votes Received by Mayoralty Candidates in First Primary Election in Atlanta, 1969

Candidate	Poor White	Working Class White	Middle Income White	Semi-Affluent White	Affluent White	Black Poor	Black Nonpoor	Total*
Millican	41.3	39.1	41.7	39.8	24.9	0.5	0.2	18.3
Cook	34.4	36.0	37.3	37.9	50.3	6.3	4.8	26.9
Tate	3.4	6.0	2.2	2.2	1.2	46.5	52.5	22.9
Massell	20.9	18.9	18.8	20.1	23.5	46.7	42.5	31.1

*Figures do not equal 100 percent because of the presence of two minor candidates. The votes for the two minor candidates were excluded from the computation of percentages by socio-economic categories.

Over 75 percent of the white voters cast their ballots for either Millican or Cook, while more than 90 percent of black voters preferred Massell or Tate. Millican, the most socially, economically, and ideologically conservative of the candidates, won pluralities in every white category except the most affluent. Given the progressive and liberal orientation of his opponents, however, Millican's showing was unimpressive. He ran far more poorly than anticoalition candidates of the past. Cook won a majority among the affluent whites, and he ran second behind Millican in all the other white categories. Despite his progressive record on minority rights issues, Cook could not compete in black neighborhoods with Tate and Massell. Tate's significantly stronger drawing power among more prosperous Negroes suggests that higher status Negroes in Atlanta placed somewhat greater emphasis upon "status" objectives than did their poorer neighbors.[17] More significant, however, was the fact that Negroes generally gave strong support to a white liberal despite the presence of a black candidate. Tate ran disastrously in white neighborhoods, while Massell made a sufficiently creditable showing to run first in the four-cornered contest. Cook finished second.

In the runoff campaign, most of the black leaders who backed Tate shifted their support to Massell, although Tate him-

[17]See James Q. Wilson, *Negro Politics: The Search for Leadership* (Glencoe, Ill.: Free Press, 1960), pp. 185–213, and Walker, "Protest and Negotiations," 109–11.

self endorsed Cook. Shortly before the election, Mayor Allen publicly entered the campaign with an attack on Massell for allegedly soliciting campaign funds improperly.[18] Generally, however, both candidates continued, as they had done in the first primary campaign, to demonstrate an impressive understanding of Atlanta's problems and to offer constructive programs for their alleviation. Sophisticated observers could detect basic differences in approach between Cook's establishment orientation and Massell's common-man–black-community orientation, but to less knowledgeable citizens, the differences surely seemed minimal. Allen's attack on Massell may well have benefited the vice mayor in lower status white neighborhoods by identifying the anti-establishment candidate.

The bulk of black voters cast their ballots for Massell, while Cook won the votes of every category of white voters by substantial margins. As Table 6–11 indicates, Massell swept to victory by receiving more than nine of every ten votes cast by Negroes and by winning approximately 28 percent of the total white vote. Cook obviously won the support of most of the voters who favored Millican in the first primary, and Massell inherited Tate's popular following.

Table 6–11

Percentage of Votes Received by Mayoralty Candidates in Runoff Primary Election in Atlanta, 1969

Candidate	Poor White	Working Class White	Middle Income White	Semi-Affluent White	Affluent White	Black Poor	Black Nonpoor	Total
Cook	66.6	67.6	73.2	72.7	73.3	8.5	6.8	45.0
Massell	33.4	32.4	26.8	27.3	26.7	91.5	93.2	55.0

Similar voting patterns appeared in the election for vice mayor. Maynard H. Jackson, the Negro lawyer who opposed Talmadge in the 1968 senatorial primary, won the office being vacated by Massell by capturing a majority of the votes in the first

[18] Three nightclub owners charged that Massell had improperly used the powers of his vice mayor's office to pressure them for campaign contributions. Mayor Allen publicly asked Massell to withdraw from the race. Massell answered with an eloquent defense in a television address.

primary election. Jackson's chief opponent was Alderman Milton G. Farris. Both candidates conducted issue-oriented campaigns, and race was never publicly a factor. Jackson, however, projected a progressive-liberal image and stood considerably to the left of Farris. Predictably, Jackson won nearly unanimous support in black precincts, and Farris piled up huge majorities in white polling places. Jackson ran behind Massell in every white voter group except in the most affluent category.

Table 6-12

Percentage of Votes Received by Vice Mayoralty Candidates in First Primary Election in Atlanta, 1969

Candidate	Poor White	Working Class White	Middle Income White	Semi-Affluent White	Affluent White	Black Poor	Black Nonpoor	Total*
Farris	72.8	68.9	73.9	73.0	65.0	1.5	1.1	39.1
Jackson	18.5	24.3	18.6	21.6	32.8	97.5	98.4	58.2

*Figures do not equal 100 percent because of the presence of two minor candidates.

The combined votes for Massell and Tate in the first primary mayoralty election, the ballots cast for Massell in the runoff, and the votes for Jackson in the vice mayoralty contest were quite similar, and all resembled the votes received by Weltner in the Fifth District general election, Jackson in the senatorial primary race, and Humphrey in the presidential contest (compare Tables 6-10, 6-11, and 6-12 with Table 6-7). In none of these elections did the progressive candidate win as much as 35 percent of the vote among any category of white voters in Atlanta. And in none did the progressive candidate (with the Massell-Tate vote combined) lose as much as 10 percent of the black vote. In Atlanta city elections, black voters packed sufficient numerical clout to win with only limited white assistance. But even in Fulton County and certainly in most other areas of the state, black voters needed substantial white assistance to provide the winning margin in an election.

In the 1968 presidential contest, a large share of the traditionally Democratic white voters joined with George Wallace, who won the bulk of the votes of the conservative coalition. Richard Nixon and Hubert Humphrey divided the ballots cast by the progressive coalition. Nixon carried the affluent white neighborhoods, and Negroes overwhelmingly voted for Humphrey. In a real sense, this three-way division permitted a rational structuring of the Georgia electorate. Wallace appealed to the traditionalist voters who rejected many of the social and ideological changes that have invaded modern Georgia. Nixon emerged as a champion of the economic progress and conservative moderation cherished by the urban bourgeoisie. Humphrey was the liberal candidate in the context of Georgia politics, and he won the support of Negroes as well as the numerically limited votes of liberal whites and loyalist Democrats. Other Georgia elections in 1968 and the 1969 city elections in Atlanta suggested a tendency on the part of the followers of both Nixon and Wallace to band together in opposition to candidates supported by the proponents of Humphrey.

In the wake of the 1968 elections, two crucial questions remained unanswered. Would substantial numbers of the traditionally Democratic Wallace voters ultimately return to the national Democratic fold? Could the Negro–affluent-white progressive coalition be restored? The answers to these questions might well determine the future of Georgia politics.

Some Trends and Prospects

Increased voter participation and the emergence of a two-party system have not contributed to the realization of the old Populist dream of a fusion of the have-nots solidified behind a program of economic and social reform.[1] Indeed, recent Georgia political history would argue that the whole notion of a northern-type New Deal politics is ludicrous when applied to Georgia. Basic elements of the New Deal coalition are absent. The state has no ethnic-religious minority with a liberal Democratic voting tradition. Georgia labor unions have been far too weak to provide the organizational framework around which members of the working class, regardless of skin color, might unite in a politics oriented toward

---

[1] Given the contemporary nature of the subject matter and the many imponderables involved, it should be noted that the following pages are no doubt colored by the author's own biases.

economics rather than race. (In 1966 only 12.7 percent of the Georgia nonagricultural work force was unionized.)[2] Political machines have existed in Georgia, but except perhaps in urban black communities, they have not performed the function of educating lower status citizens to the relationship between politics and bread-and-butter issues that northern machines have sometimes done. But more important than these institutional factors in thwarting New Deal political alignments is the *Weltanschauung* of the major voting groups in the state.

The lower status whites are simply Georgia's most politically conservative people. Racist in social attitudes, fundamentalist in religion, provincial in outlook, the whites in the countryside and in the less affluent urban neighborhoods have tended to place their reliance upon tradition and folk custom. Politically, they have been nurtured on a blend of Talmadgism and the county unit system. The south and central Georgia countryside, the rural areas of north Georgia, and the lower status white districts in the cities have been the most consistently conservative areas in the state. In recent elections, north Georgia townsmen have tended to vote with the conservative coalition, whereas an increasing Negro vote has tempered, though it has not basically changed, the conservative domination of black belt politics. Broadly, the rural–small-town–poorer-urban white coalition commands approximately 45 percent of Georgia's vote. Marvin Griffin won almost 40 percent in the 1962 gubernatorial primary; Maddox won 54 percent in the 1966 runoff primary and 46 percent in the general election; and Wallace carried 43 percent in his presidential effort. While gradually declining numerically in relation to the rest of the population, the conservative coalition represents a formidable and a cohesive bloc of votes.

The least likely allies for the conservative whites are the Negroes. Black and rural–small-town–lower-status whites are the most racially conscious of all voters. Although both black and white lower class citizens are economically liberal in a technical sense, in practice economic issues rarely fail to possess racial overtones. For example, Negroes have overwhelmingly approved of the federal poverty program, while the bulk of poverty-level whites

[2] U.S. Department of Labor, *News*, January 19, 1966.

have disapproved on the grounds that it was oriented toward Negroes.[3] As Professor Alfred O. Hero has reported: "Federal welfare programs have benefited Negroes disproportionately since they have been the most economically deprived group in the region, and the racially conservative informants were often concerned that there would be hidden, if not overt, liberal racial and social reform strings attached to federal money."[4] The substantial majorities lower status whites in the cities awarded Barry Goldwater, who would certainly rank as one of the more economically conservative candidates to appear on a Georgia ballot in recent years, evidenced the relative values that poorer whites placed on economic liberalism and white supremacy. Negroes have tended to identify with the federal government. "No other group ever has had to look to government for so much assistance affecting such vital interests as Negro Americans must at present," Professor Everett C. Ladd has observed.[5] Lower status whites, on the other hand, have not only been belligerently hostile to federal minority rights measures, but they also are apt to be generally anti-establishment in a Maddox-Wallace sense of the term.

Politically, black citizens have consistently been Georgia's most liberal voters. Although Negroes make up little more than 18 percent of the state's registered voters, their solidarity is greater than that of any other general voting group. The combined votes of Negroes and liberal whites account for some 25 percent of the total Georgia vote. Ellis Arnall received 29 percent in the first gubernatorial primary in 1966; Maynard Jackson won 23 percent in his effort to unseat Senator Talmadge; and Humphrey got 27 percent of the vote in the 1968 presidential election.

The urban-suburban bourgeoisie form the core of the remaining 30 percent of the total vote in Georgia. General Eisenhower won just over 30 percent of the state's vote in 1952, when Republicanism was yet to become fashionable. In 1968 Nixon won just over 30 percent against opponents on both the left and the right. Politically, these voters stood between the Negroes and the ordinary whites. While endorsing law and order and social stabil-

[3] Brink and Harris, *Black and White*, p. 134.

[4] Hero, *The Southerner and World Affairs*, p. 374.

[5] Everett C. Ladd, Jr., *Negro Political Leadership in the South* (Ithaca, N.Y.: Cornell University Press, 1966), pp. 36–37.

ity, they were not noticeably devoted to segregation and white supremacy. While economically conservative, they also favored economic and civic progress and accepted the legitimacy of governmental intervention in the regulation of some economic activities and in the provision of social services. The more affluent urban-suburban whites approved of state's rights, but unlike other white Georgians, they were urban rather than rurally oriented.

Had the rural–small-town–lower-status whites been described as reactionary, then the urban-suburban whites could properly be termed conservative. Since the followers of Wallace and Maddox have been referred to in this work as conservatives, however, the affluent whites can best be described as progressives. Negroes have behaved politically as liberals. In the very broadest sense, consequently, 45 percent of Georgia's total vote is conservative; 30 percent is progressive; and 25 percent is liberal. These divisions should, of course, be regarded with the greatest caution. Not only do myriad factors influence the way an individual actually casts his vote, but the voting blocs described here are crude and general groupings. Yet, the consistency of these alignments suggests that they are substantially the voting foundations upon which political competition in Georgia rests.

The divergent political inclinations of the three main voting coalitions are sure to strain the newly emergent two-party system in the state. It is probable that Georgia politics in the future will be shaken by predominately black write-in movements (such as the 1966 "Write In Georgia" campaign for Arnall), predominately black independent political activities (such as the Freedom Democratic Party in Mississippi and the National Democratic Party in Alabama), and conservative white third-party movements (such as the 1968 Wallace campaign). In November, 1969, the Georgia Voters League, a predominately Negro organization, held a statewide convention to nominate a gubernatorial candidate for the 1970 election. More than 2,000 Negroes, including many prominent civil rights leaders, attended from throughout the state.[6] The convention nominated C. B. King, a black civil rights lawyer from Albany, for governor and a slate of candidates for other offices. As this is being written, it is still unclear whether the Georgia Voters

[6] Bill Montgomery, in the Atlanta *Constitution*, November 30, 1969; Sam Hopkins, in *ibid.*, December 12, 1969.

League and the newly formed Coalition of Black Leaders intend to enter their candidates in the Democratic primary or in the general election. The extent of the movement's popular support among Negroes generally is also unclear. Similarly, the American Independent party has announced its intention to enter a Wallace-oriented candidate in the 1970 general election for governor. The potential significance of these actions is obvious enough. But barring a radical and improbable restructuring of the framework of national political institutions, Georgia voters will presumably come to terms with a two-party system.

In the past, the basic alliances in state politics pitted Negroes and the more affluent urban whites against the rural–small-town–lower-status whites. Talmadge–anti-Talmadge Democratic factionalism rested upon such alliances. Blacks and affluent whites found common cause in opposition to rural domination of state politics and in support of progressive urban government. The rivalries fostered by the county unit system tended to suppress the social and economic divisions between black poor and white wealthy. But the racial liberalism and welfare economic policies favored by Negroes, and the racial moderation and economic conservatism preferred by affluent whites, were significant attitudinal differences that militated against the stability of the alliance.

The breakdown of the county unit system and the rise of two-party competition brought these differences to a head. White affluents identified with the Republican party, and the Georgia G.O.P. established its voter base in the more prestigious residential areas of city and suburb. During the 1950's, Atlanta area Republicans attempted with substantial success to attract Negro support. But during the 1960's Negroes increasingly found the national Democratic party more to their liking, while Georgia Republicans shifted to a "lily white" strategy. The Republicans sought to hold the affluent whites with economic conservatism and to attract the less socially and economically privileged whites with social conservatism. This strategy has proved successful on a number of occasions. Goldwater swept all before him except the black precincts and the north Georgia countryside. In city elections in Savannah and Columbus and in congressional elections in the Atlanta area, Republicans have solidified the white vote behind the G.O.P. banner. Assuming the absence of a viable Wallace-type third party alternative, it seems probable that future Republican presidential candidates can expect substantial support from rural–small-town–lower-status white voters. Nixon, not Humphrey, was Wallace's principal competitor for votes from the conservative coalition in 1968. A South-wide Oliver Quayle poll conducted for NBC News shortly before the 1968 election found that an overwhelming majority of pro-Wallace respondents stated a preference for Nixon over Humphrey. With Wallace out of the race, 68 percent of his supporters said that they would vote for Nixon, whereas 12 percent informed Quayle's pollsters that they would shift to Humphrey. (Of the remaining 20 percent, 15 percent stated that they would simply refuse to vote if Wallace were not on the ballot and 5 percent answered "not sure.")[7] More recently, the Nixon Administration, and especially Vice President Spiro T. Agnew, has, appearances would indicate, strengthened the Republican cause among members of the conservative coalition in Georgia. Studies have clearly demonstrated that voters rarely change their party identification, but recent years have not been normal ones in Georgia politics. In 1968, for example, substantial numbers of lower status Atlanta whites apparently voted Democratic (for Senator Talmadge), Independent (for Wallace), and Republican (for Fletcher Thompson) on the same ballot. This kind of issue orientation suggests that party identification may not be an accurate guide to Georgia voting behavior.[8]

The Republican adoption of a "lily white" strategy has placed considerable strain on the Democrats. The Democrats successfully countered the G.O.P. threat to Democratic control of the governorship in 1966 with the nomination of Lester Maddox. State's rights candidates such as Maddox, Wallace, and Talmadge have for the most part been able to turn back the Republican assault on the conservative coalition. But a Democratic strategy based on rural–small-town–lower-status white votes requires either an extremely strong candidate or a weak opposition to produce a majority. The Talmadge faction relied more upon the county unit

[7] Oliver Quayle Poll for NBC News, results made available to the author through the courtesy of NBC News Elections.

[8] On party identification and voting behavior, see Key, *Public Opinion and American Democracy*, pp. 294–301, and Matthews and Prothro, *New Southern Politics*, pp. 369–404.

system and a divided opposition than it did upon the ability to command the support of a voting majority. Except in the case of such entrenched Democrats as Senators Talmadge and Russell, the candidates who have overwhelmed the opposition in recent years have been Governors Vandiver and Sanders, and they did so with the support of the progressive coalition.

This situation leaves open several alternatives. If the Republicans succeed in uniting the bulk of white voters, Georgia would again become a one-party state. The Second Reconstruction would be followed by the rule of Bourbon Democrats, this time calling themselves Republicans. Given the vast economic and demographic changes that have swept over Georgia during the twentieth century, such a prospect might appear implausible. Nevertheless, it is a very real possibility. White Georgians have in the past responded irrationally to the threat of Negroes' holding the political balance of power, and it is by no means certain that they will not do so again. The second alternative would be the long term domination of the Democratic party by the state's rights Democrats. In that event, Georgia voters would have their choice between two conservative parties. Such an eventuality would seem feasible, however, only if black voters isolated themselves in a third party. Finally, a third alternative is that the Democrats will ultimately have to make a major effort to restore the progressive coalition. A moderately progressive Democrat could count on the votes of Negroes, would be in a favorable position to recapture the north Georgia towns, and would have to make a substantial showing in affluent urban-suburban neighborhoods. The willingness of the Macon upper class to support a Democrat in the 1967 mayoralty election suggests that affluent whites in that city are not irrevocably committed to Republicanism. The disintegration of the black–affluent-white coalition in the recent city elections in Atlanta, however, demonstrated the magnitude of the problem the Democrats would face. In any case, the most promising conclusion that can be made about the future of Georgia voting patterns is that the conservative-progressive voting coalitions are apt to prove more permanent than party identification. Or, to put it another way, the best that can be hoped is that Georgia politics will not become substantially more conservative than it has been in the past.

List of Tables

LIST OF TABLES

Index